C. FRED BERGSTEN
IL SAKONG
Editors

Korea–United States Cooperation in the New World Order

Institute for International Economics
Washington, DC
Institute for Global Economics
Seoul, Korea
February 1996

C. Fred Bergsten is Director of the Institute for International Economics, Chairman of the Competitiveness Policy Council, and Chairman of the APEC Eminent Persons Group. He was Assistant Secretary for International Affairs of the US Treasury (1977–81); Assistant for International Economic Affairs to the National Security Council (1969–71); and a Senior Fellow at the Brookings Institution (1972–76), the Carnegie Endowment for International Peace (1981), and the Council on Foreign Relations (1967–68). He is the author or editor of 22 books on a wide range of international economic issues including *The Political Economy of United States-Korea Cooperation* with Il SaKong (1995), *Reconcilable Differences? United States–Japan Economic Conflict* with Marcus Noland (1993), *Pacific Dynamism and the International Economic System* with Marcus Noland (1993), *America in the World Economy: A Strategy for the 1990s* (1988), *Trade Policy in the 1980s* with William Cline (1984), *American Multinationals and American Interests* (1978), *The Dilemmas of the Dollar* (1976), and *World Politics and International Economics* (1975).

Il SaKong is currently Chairman and CEO of the Institute for Global Economics. He has been Special Consultant to the International Monetary Fund in Washington, DC since 1989 and is a member of the Korea-US Wisemen Council and Cohost of the Korea-US Twenty-First Century Council. Dr. SaKong also served in the government of the Republic of Korea as Minister of Finance (1987–88), Senior Secretary to the President for Economic Affairs (1983–87), Senior Counsellor to the Minister of Economic Planning Board (1982), and Senior Economist of the Presidential Council on Economic and Scientific Affairs (1979–80). Dr. SaKong was Senior Fellow, Research Director, and Vice President at the Korea Development Institute (KDI) and was President of the Korea Institute for Industrial Economics and Trade (KIET). He has written/edited eight books and numerous articles in professional journals dealing with the Korean economy, major issues in economic development, and international finance and trade policy issues, including *The Political Economy of United States–Korea Cooperation* with C. Fred Bergsten (1995), and *Korea in the World Economy*, (1993).

INSTITUTE FOR INTERNATIONAL ECONOMICS
11 Dupont Circle, NW
Washington, DC 20036-1207
(202) 328-9000   FAX: (202) 328-0900
http://www.iie.com

C. Fred Bergsten, *Director*
Christine F. Lowry, *Director of Publications*

Typesetting by Sandra F. Watts
Printing by Automated Graphic Systems

Printed in the United States of America
98 97 96   5 4 3 2 1

ISBN 0-88132-226-1

Marketed and Distributed outside the USA and Canada by Longman Group UK Limited, London

Contents

III Korea–US Cooperation in the Asia Pacific

Appendices

Preface

This volume derives from the second meeting of the Korea–United States Twenty-First Century Council meeting in February 1995. The Council was created by the Institute for International Economics in Washington and the Institute for Global Economics in Seoul to provide an ongoing forum to discuss economic and overall relations between Korea and the United States. It brings together top government officials, former officials, private-sector leaders, and policy-oriented researchers. The initial session of the Council took place in February 1994 and produced the volume *The Political Economy of Korea–United States Cooperation*, also edited by ourselves.

The focus of the conference, and thus of this book, is threefold: the security and overall political context for the relationship between Korea and the United States, the bilateral economic relationship, and cooperation between the two countries in the broader multilateral, especially regional, economic context. Leading experts from the two countries introduced each topic with papers that are reproduced here. The Council will hold its third meeting in February 1996, and we look forward to another lively and valuable discussion of this relationship, which is increasingly critical to both countries and to the world economy as a whole.

The Institute for International Economics is a private nonprofit institution for the study and discussion of international economic policy. Its purpose is to analyze important issues in that area and to develop and communicate practical new approaches for dealing with them. The Institute is completely nonpartisan.

The Institute is funded largely by philanthropic foundations. Major institutional grants are now being received from the German Marshall Fund of the United States, which created the Institute with a generous commitment of funds in 1981, and from the Ford Foundation, the Korea Foundation, the Andrew Mellon Foundation, and the C. V. Starr Foundation. A number of other foundations and private corporations also contribute to the highly diversified financial resources of the Institute. The GE Foundation, Inc., provided additional support for this study. About 12 percent of the Institute's resources in our latest fiscal year were provided by contributors outside the United States, including about 5 percent from Japan.

The Board of Directors bears overall responsibility for the Institute and gives general guidance and approval to its research program—including identification of topics that are likely to become important to international economic policymakers over the medium run (generally, one to three years), and which thus should be addressed by the Institute. The Director, working closely with the staff and outside Advisory Committee, is responsible for the development of particular projects and makes the final decision to publish an individual study.

The Institute hopes that its studies and other activities will contribute to building a stronger foundation for international economic policy around the world. We invite readers of these publications to let us know how they think we can best accomplish this objective.

The Institute for Global Economics is based in Seoul, Korea. It is a private, nonprofit institution that was established with two basic objectives. The first is to provide a forum for both Korean and international leaders in academia, government, business, and journalism to discuss international issues of common interest and Korea's role in the world community. The second objective is to conduct global issue-oriented research to (1) suggest alternative strategies and policies for both the Korean government and business firms to adapt to the rapidly changing international economic and technological environment, and (2) to draw attention to worldwide issues.

The Institute for Global Economics is financed by annual donations by private corporations and membership fees from business corporations as well as individuals. In addition, several of the Institute's projects are funded by public foundations. The Korea–United States 21st Century Council is partially supported by the Korea Foundation, which took the initiative in proposing the project.

IL SAKONG
Chairman
Institute for Global Economics

C. FRED BERGSTEN
Director
Institute for International Economics
January 1996

1

Introduction

C. FRED BERGSTEN AND IL SAKONG

The Korea–United States Twenty-First Century Council held its second meeting in Washington in February 1995. The Council brings together top government officials, former officials, members of the legislatures, business leaders, and scholars from the two countries. Its purpose is to assess both the bilateral relationship between the countries and their differing perspectives on key global problems. The Council again met for two full days and discussed a rich agenda of wide-ranging topics.

As at its first meeting in early 1994, whose results we published later that year under the title *The Political Economy of Korea–United States Cooperation*, the Council divided its meeting into three major components. The focus of the group is on economic issues, but it believes that they must always be seen in the broader political and security context. Hence the first component of the program addressed security issues, especially as affected by the flare-up of the nuclear issue in 1994 and the Geneva accord that attempted to resolve it. A particular focus was the position of North Korea, in light of the leadership change in that country and its desperate economic conditions, and the outlook for relations between North and South Korea.

With that background in place, the Council turned to economic issues. Here the focus was a continuation of the lively debates that characterized the Council's first meeting: Was Korea serious about liberalization and globalization of its economy? Was the United States determined to pursue an "aggressive unilateralist" approach to pry open markets in Korea (and elsewhere in Asia)? How could companies in the two coun-

C. Fred Bergsten is director of the Institute for International Economics. Il SaKong is director of the Institute for Global Economics.

tries work together more effectively, both in penetrating each others' markets and——perhaps even more importantly—in third markets?

A particular focus was the proper mix of bilateral, regional, and global strategies for the governments of the two countries to pursue. The Council addressed these alternatives systematically. Considerable attention was paid to the results so far of President Kim Young Sam's globalization strategy and of the Dialogue for Economic Cooperation that the two countries had pursued over the previous year. In light of the dramatic results of the 1994 APEC summit at Bogor, Indonesia, special attention was paid to the prospects for APEC as a regional venue for Korea–United States cooperation—and the possibility that such cooperation could play a central role in translating APEC's bold vision into operational success.

Just a few weeks before this second meeting of the Council, a new political situation arose in the United States with the election in November 1994 of a Republican Congress. Would this development significantly alter the basis in America for the relationship with Korea? A spirited discussion of the topic was led by Congressman Doug Bereuter, the new chairman of the Asia and Pacific Subcommittee of the International Relations Committee of the House of Representatives, and thus one of the key members of Congress on the relevant set of issues.

The Presentations

As the first speaker of the first session, which dealt with Korean reunification issues, Kim Hakjoon examines North Korea's geopolitical position vis-à-vis its neighbors and the United States following the Geneva nuclear accord of October 1994. Despite some remaining obstacles, Kim asserts that the accord will enable North Korea to engage in a "fundamental effort" to improve its relations with the United States and Japan. In order to counterbalance this tendency, North Korea's other two neighbors, China and Russia, will continue to try to exert their influence on the affairs of the peninsula.

Under these circumstances, South Korea must reorient its North Korea policy. The South Korean government must be ready to adopt a more positive stance, moving away from containment and placing priority on the North-South dialogue in order to begin building mutual trust. Implementing the existing North-South agreement reached in 1991 would be a vital first step in this regard.

Analyzing the prospects for economic integration in the Korean peninsula, Young-Sun Lee first looks at the current economic conditions in North Korea. His calculations, based on the latest statistics, reveal that due to consecutive years of negative growth, the North Korean economy has shrunk by as much as 30 percent since the end of the 1980s. Although the resulting hardships on the general population have been creating pressures for change, Lee notes that many scholars are skeptical about North Korea's ability and willingness to undertake Chinese-style reforms in the foreseeable future. Nevertheless, some sort of reform involving the opening of the economy will be inevitable.

Lee then considers the costs and benefits of economic integration. While the burden on the South Korean people would be high and would depend on different unification scenarios, the benefits conferred on the North would far outweigh the costs. In the current political climate, however, integration efforts would have to remain limited to trade and investment, and even these activities continue to be severely restrained. More needs to be done to foster exchanges at the nongovernmental level and help the North promote multilateral cooperation with the United States and Japan.

As the US speaker, Robert Zoellick begins with an observation of North Korea, which he finds to be in serious economic trouble, isolated from the world community, and going through an uncertain political transition. While the country remains prone to violence, Zoellick does not believe that it is "out of control or suicidal" but is well aware of what its interests and objectives are. Zoellick also believes that because of many potential ambiguities, the nuclear agreement between the United States and North Korea will take a long time to implement.

Against this background, Zoellick makes a number of suggestions for the United States and South Korea in dealing with North Korea in an effective and concerted manner. For instance, while both the United States and South Korea have chosen the strategy of engagement, the North must know that it could face containment at any time. Most importantly, in its dealings with other major countries, the North must never be allowed to circumvent the South. A more aggressive approach to economic liberalization on the part of South Korea is also critical. By reducing distortions in the domestic economy, the South will be better prepared for reunification and enjoy greater political support from other countries.

In the second session, on the Korean-US economic relationship, Daniel Tarullo argues that the most important factor in future relations is how Korea resolves its ambivalence: globalization and liberalization is necessary for continued growth but is also a threat to policies that have served the country well. While the Kim Young Sam administration has placed great emphasis and priority on economic reform, there has been little progress, especially in the area of foreign investment. Similarly, the newly created Dialogue for Economic Cooperation, endorsed by the presidents of both countries, has had only modest success, as Korea remains one of the least attractive places to foreign investors in Asia. Resistance by lower levels of bureaucracies and the public at large continues to be the main obstacle. Overcoming these obstacles, and thus the ambivalence, should be of greatest concern to the Korean government.

In examining Korean-US economic relations in the 1990s, Soogil Young observes that unlike the 1980s, which was characterized by often-severe trade tensions between Korea and the United States, the 1990s have thus far been without major conflict. Potential sources of friction have not disappeared, however, and with the end of the Uruguay Round, Young believes that the United States will turn its attention to bilateral issues again. The United States is also likely to choose a confrontational approach to dealing with trade barriers, as is already evident in the case concerning access to the Korean automobile market.

Such an approach will not reduce or eliminate nontariff barriers in Korea and instead will provoke a backlash and perhaps even a trade war. Korea must remove the barriers on its own, particularly those of a regulatory nature, and it knows it must do so quickly. In the era of globalization, both countries must reorient their respective strategies so as to develop as partners in Northeast Asia. One critical step in this direction would be to begin examining the possibility of a free trade agreement between the two countries.

Doug Bereuter, the newly appointed chairman of the Asia and Pacific Subcommittee in the US House of Representatives, offers a congressional perspective on Korean-US cooperation. Bereuter is very clear about his concerns and intentions regarding the US-Korean economic relationship. Unlike his predecessors, he intends to place a higher priority on economic issues, and Korea is at the top of his list. Bereuter expresses serious concern over Korea's nontariff barriers, which are not limited to agricultural products and are not unlike those that existed in Japan a decade ago. With the end of the Cold War, Bereuter believes that the United States "can and should demand an end to the unfair treatment" for American exporters to Korea.

In the final session, dealing with Korean-US cooperation in the Asia Pacific Economic Cooperation forum (APEC), C. Fred Bergsten assesses the future of APEC by first reviewing the results of the Bogor Declaration. Though not a binding agreement, the Bogor Declaration, as the largest trade agreement in history, is significant for the political commitment that it represents. Bergsten also notes that the de facto target date for free trade in the region would in fact be sooner than 2020, since the fast-track countries whose target date is the year 2010 would represent 85 to 90 percent of the trade liberalization. The aggregate payoff of free trade in APEC is expected to be enormous, increasing world output by nearly $400 billion by 2010, according to one study.

To be sure, a variety of challenges remain. Bergsten lists three of them: determining which countries would be on the fast track, the coverage of liberalization, and the treatment of nonmembers. A technical issue is the format of the negotiation, which Bergsten suggests should be done on the basis of unilateral offers by each country rather than "face-to-face negotiations" involving all members. As for Korea and the United States,

Bergsten believes that achieving free trade through APEC would be far superior to a bilateral agreement or Korean accession to NAFTA, for it avoids problems of discrimination against other countries.

Jang-Hee Yoo and Taeho Bark examine Korean-US economic cooperation within the context of APEC. While many foresee a tripolar world economic system emerging, Yoo and Bark believe that the emergence of APEC will lead to a bipolar system consisting of Europe and the Asia Pacific. And as long as "sound and constructive" regionalism is maintained, they see no reason a new international economic order, free of instability and conflict and based on open multilateralism, cannot prevail.

In order for such an order to emerge, APEC must develop accordingly. Skeptics point to at least two obstacles: the political and economic gap between developed and developing countries within APEC and the region's heterogeneity. However, Korean-US economic cooperation over the past several decades demonstrates why such skepticism may be unwarranted. Despite the differences in culture and level of development and despite some remaining trade issues, the two countries' economic relationship has been a model of cooperation. To be sure, the relationship is at an important crossroad. But by shifting the focus to industrial, technological, and research cooperation, Korea and the United States could continue to serve as a model for APEC.

SECURITY AND ECONOMIC
IMPLICATIONS OF REUNIFICATION

2

North-South Relations
after the Nuclear Accord

HAKJOON KIM

Aftermath of the Nuclear Accord

On 18 October 1994 it was announced that agreement had been reached between US Ambassador-at-Large Robert Gallucci and the North Korean representative, First Vice Foreign Minister Kang Sok-ju, on a nuclear accord between the United States and North Korea at the third stage of the third round of high-level talks. With the formal signing of the document on 21 October at Geneva, and for the first time since North Korea announced its intention to withdraw from the Nuclear Non-Proliferation Treaty (NPT) on 12 March 1993, the often tedious, long, drawn-out North Korean nuclear issue appeared to be settled for the time being.

The accord between North Korea and the United States contained the following important points of agreement:

■ Vital components of two light-water reactors were to be transferred to the North, and all safety measures required by the International

Hakjoon Kim received his Ph.D. in political science from the University of Pittsburgh in 1972. Dr. Kim was chairman and professor in the Department of Political Science, Seoul National University, and an Alexander von Humboldt Foundation Fellow at the University of Munich and the University of Vienna, respectively. He was a member of the National Assembly, and served as chief press secretary and spokesman for the president of the Republic of Korea. In 1993–94 he was a guest scholar at the Woodrow Wilson International Center for Scholars. At present, he is chairman of the Board of Trustees, Dankook University, Seoul.

Atomic Energy Agency (IAEA) were to be implemented. North Korea agreed to abide by the terms of the NPT. With the North's assent to these provisions, the path was in effect cleared for IAEA special inspections.

■ The North agreed to dismantle all facilities and structures related to its nuclear production and to transfer its spent fuel rods to a third country.

■ Three months from the date of the agreement, crude oil was to have been provided to the North as an alternative energy source. Crude oil was to be provided until the light-water reactor installation.

■ The North agreed to the implementation of its joint declaration with the South on the nonnuclearization of the peninsula, and the resumption of North-South dialogue is stipulated.

■ North Korea was to receive light-water nuclear reactors with a total capacity of 2,000 megawatts. To facilitate this, an international consortium was to be established, and South Korea and the United States agreed that all efforts would be made to assure that the light-water reactors be of the "South Korean type."

■ The United States agreed to rescind some restrictions on trade and investment in North Korea and was in due course to exchange liaison offices with the North (*Korea Times*, 19, 21, and 22 October 1994).

In examining the accord, critics have argued that its provisions are all to the benefit of North Korea, that the United States has yielded far too much, or that in the end South Korea is responsible for the entire financial burden of providing for the light-water reactors. Certainly it is difficult to refute the assertion that North Korea is the greatest beneficiary. This is because North Korea has managed, in exchange for guaranteeing its nuclear transparency—an obligation it owes to the international community in any event—to lay down the stepping stones for ultimately establishing diplomatic relations with the United States through the exchange of liaison offices but also, in effect, to secure two light-water nuclear reactors for free.

However, it is rather shortsighted to say that the United States and South Korea are on the short end of the stick. For the immediate future, the transparency of North Korea's nuclear program has been secured, and, while it will be a few years down the road, the way for nuclear inspections has been cleared. Securing this transparency was, of course, extremely important; thus, one major goal of the negotiations was achieved. In this vein, Hans Blic, IAEA director general, noted that the Geneva accord would help ease some of the world community's concerns with North Korea's nuclear intentions.

In addition, it may appear that South Korea has suffered some sort of comparative loss with the so-called success the North appears to have garnered in easing its three major points of Angst: the succession of power, severe economic hardship, and international isolation. But in the long run, the results for the South are not entirely negative. It is true that the light-water reactors will cost approximately $4 billion. This is no small sum, but with the prospect of reunification with a North that faces severe energy shortages, the South would have had to spend this money in any event to alleviate the problem. Further, the improvement of US–North Korean relations would have been a necessary step on the road to unification anyway. Therefore, in examining the results of the accord, we need a detailed examination of what changes will occur in the reunification climate as a result of the agreement rather than getting hung up in calculations of possible benefits and losses of those affected.

On the surface, this agreement had three major components: the freezing of the North Korean nuclear program, the improvement of US–North Korean relations, and the resumption of North-South dialogue.

The strategic targets of the United States were extension of the NPT regime at a global conference held in April 1995 and the freezing of North Korea's nuclear program. These have been achieved. In addition, the US–North Korean nuclear agreement became an international accord, as the 15-member United Nations Security Council formally endorsed it in a unanimous vote on 4 November 1994. This endorsement cleared the way for the IAEA to verify that North Korea has frozen its nuclear program. Noting that the agreement contains pledges to the international community, the Security Council statement implied that if the North failed to honor them, it could face international sanctions.

On the other hand, for South Korea the most important variable influencing its relations with the North is the stipulation establishing a liaison office between North Korea and the United States. This is both an important opportunity for the North to join the international community and ultimately the factor that will spur the North to greater openness and greater respect for international society.

Once the liaison office is established and before full diplomatic relations are achieved, the issues of North Korea's human rights violations, its missile exports, and its weapons of mass destruction must be resolved. This process will likely take considerable time and will be accompanied by other vicissitudes and complications.

In addition, full diplomatic relations with the United States must await full resolution of the technical problems that will arise in the process of guaranteeing the North's nuclear transparency, as well as the inevitable procedural delays within the United States' own legal system and complications in the relationship between the Clinton administration and Congress. Thus considerable time will be necessary on this front also.

There are several specific impediments to the recognition of North

Korea. From the US point of view, the North falls into the categories of terrorist nation, nation with a history of human rights violations, and communist country that thereby runs afoul of US laws on "trading with the enemy," with the consequent restrictions on US exports of weapons and high technology.

In order to relax these restrictions on contacts with North Korea, US domestic law must be amended through cooperation between the administrative and legislative branches of the government. Yet after the November 1994 mid-term elections, the Republican Party gained control of both the Senate and the House of Representatives. This promises to make cooperation between the two branches of government an even more arduous process. The leaders of the Republican Party have already been critical of the Clinton administration's handling of foreign policy in general and its North Korean policy in specific. Republicans have strongly and quite publicly expressed their unhappiness with the Geneva accord.[1]

Subsequently, an incident occurred that might have scuttled the diplomatic progress between North Korea and the United States. When the American OH-58 Kiowa helicopter inadvertently strayed into North Korea's airspace on 17 December 1994, the North shot it down, killing one pilot and capturing the other. The Clinton administration worked through the United Nations and private channels as well as using the Korean War truce in an attempt to solve the issue. By 30 December, North Korea had handed over the body of the killed pilot and freed his co-pilot Bobby Hall. To get this settlement, the United States signed an agreement with North Korea under which the United States expressed sincere regret for the incident and agreed "to maintain military contact in the appropriate forum to identify and take measures for preventing occurrences that threaten peace and security on the Korea peninsula" (*Korea Times*, 31 December 1994).

In this process, there was one important development: North Korea refused to use the Military Armistice Commission as a channel for negotiations. If a meeting of the commission had been called, then South Korea could have participated. In order to exclude South Korean participation, North Korea strongly argued for bilateral negotiations with the United States, which finally agreed. And so US deputy assistant secretary of state in charge of East Asian and Pacific affairs, Thomas Hubbard, visited Pyongyang—the first high-ranking incumbent government official to do so. This case boosted North Korea's assertion that "bilateral negotiations between North Korea and the United States should be started

---

1. For example, see former US Secretary of the State James Baker's testimony before the House International Relations Committee on 13 January 1995 and on 15 January 1995. He criticized the accord as an abrupt change from a carrot-and-stick to a carrot-only policy. "And given its history, I do not think this is going to work with North Korea," he added.

for an ultimate peace agreement between North Korea and the United States" (*Korea Times*, 31 December 1994).

Against this backdrop, one may ask what was meant by the phrase "military contact in the appropriate forum" in the context of existing relations between the United States and North Korea. The United States officially interpreted it to mean "at the Military Armistice Commission." However, Seoul interpreted it to mean that North Korea had secured one more avenue leading to Washington. As one Korean newspaper put it, "This could be a significant diplomatic achievement for the North, which has consistently sought to shove South Korea aside in its approach toward Washington" (*Korea Times*, 31 December 1994).

Then, on 9 January 1995, North Korea said it was opening its ports to US shipping and cargo, just after a South Korean company announced it would send the first consignment of American oil to North Korea. The landmark announcement by North Korea's Foreign Ministry spokesman said, "The restrictions on the import of United States commodities and the ban on the entry of United States trading ships into North Korean ports will be lifted by mid-January." He called the move a "part of the work for the full normalization of political and economic relations with the United States" (*Korea Times*, 10 January 1995).

In compliance with the Geneva accord, on 20 January 1995 the United States agreed to permit direct telephone links with North Korea as part of a modest package of steps toward initial easing of the 45-year-old trade curbs on North Korea. In a move that could mean $5 million to $10 million a year for Pyongyang, American businesses were permitted to import North Korean magnetite, a rare metal used to coat the insides of steel-industry blast furnaces. American news organizations were to be allowed for the first time to open offices in North Korea and North Korean journalists to set up shop in the United States. Also, American visitors to North Korea were to be permitted to make unlimited credit-card purchases in connection with personal travel. North Korea were to be permitted to clear financial transactions not beginning or terminating in the United States. An unspecified portion of the $11 million in North Korean-related assets frozen in the United States was to be unfrozen. Also, American firms were to be considered on a case-by-case basis for participation in the $4.5 billion US-led project to provide North Korea with new light-water nuclear reactors and alternative energy supplies. Finally, in January 1995 the first consignment of oil promised by the United States to North Korea as part of its nuclear deal arrived in a North Korean port (*Korea Times*, 22 January 1995).

On another front, North Korean and US experts held talks in Berlin on 28–31 January 1995 on the details of the light-water reactors. It was also reported that North Korea was quite helpful to American experts who were checking the chemical state of spent fuel rods taken from the Yongbyon-based atomic reactor (*Korea Times*, 29 January 1995).

Prospects for Japanese Diplomatic
Recognition of North Korea

The resolution of the nuclear issue and North Korea's apparent willingness to compromise on the issue of negotiations for US diplomatic recognition also provide a foundation for rapid normalization of relations between North Korea and Japan. The Japanese government has recognized this opportunity. Immediately after the announcement of the Geneva agreement, Minister of Foreign Affairs Kono Yahei commented, "One obstacle has been reduced. Once the procedures for ratifying the accord between the United States and North Korea are completed, that will be the point where we can resume talks with the North." He expressed his government's strong desire to resume talks on diplomatic recognition. In addition, Prime Minister Murayama Tomiichi indicated that his government would make strong efforts to normalize relations with North Korea in 1995.

Japan has traditionally linked security on the Korean peninsula to its own security and thus seeks to extend its influence there. The talks on diplomatic recognition were one avenue for pursuing its goals. However, North Korean–Japanese talks on diplomatic recognition broke down in November 1992 over the issue of the return to Japan of Kim Hyun-hee's language instructor, Lee Un-hae. Kim Hyun-hee, a female North Korean hijacker of a Korean Air jet in 1987, confessed to the South Korean authorities that she had learned Japanese from Lee Un-hae, who according to her was "a woman kidnapped from Japan." The Japanese government concluded that Kim Hyun-hee's confession was factual, but the North categorically denied the accusation. And despite the controversy over North Korea's nuclear programs, it is known that up until 23 August 1994 there were at least five rounds of unofficial contact between diplomatic representatives from both sides in Beijing.

Discussions between Japan and North Korea have been impeded by such obstacles as North Korea's nuclear program, reparations, Japan's view of past history in the region, and the issue of Lee Un-hae. However, with the resolution of the North Korean nuclear issue, the greatest obstacle to improving relations between the two countries has been removed. The issue of reparations to North Korea remains blocked by serious differences, but in the end this will not be a major obstacle. Aside from this, other problems seem to be of a chiefly moral nature (e.g., Japanese distortions of modern history and the Lee Un-hae issue).

But with the removal of the largest obstacle to talks on diplomatic recognition, elements for promoting the talks have increased. Because North Korea desperately needs Japanese economic assistance for the stability of the Kim Jung Il regime and as a way of solving its economic difficulties, North Korea may well be willing to modify its stance on Japanese–North Korean diplomatic relations. The fact that Prime Minister Murayama is a member of the Social Democratic Party of Japan (formerly the Japan Socialist Party), a party that has maintained close ties with North Korea, should also foster an early rapprochement between North Korea and Japan. And in fact on 16 January 1995, North Korea's official organ, the *Rodong Sinmum* (Worker's Newspaper), carried a statement from its Foreign Ministry indicating it might be ready to resume talks with Japan. Japan responded favorably. On 20 January, Foreign Minister Kon Yohei urged North Korea to reopen talks to try and normalize relations between the two countries (*Korea Times*, 22 January 1995).

The chances are that North Korea will use the diplomatic recognition it receives from Japan to leverage an acceleration in diplomatic recognition from the United States. But even if Japan plays its North Korean "card" this way, South Koreans need not perceive such developments as having a negative influence on Japanese relations with them. As an established Japan specialist has persuasively argued, "If properly handled, the establishment of diplomatic ties between Japan and North Korea can contribute to peace and stability on the Korean peninsula by finalizing cross recognition of the two Koreas by the four major powers" (Hongnack Kim 1994, 694).

The Effect on North-South Relations

As discussed above, one of the direct results of the resolution of the North Korean nuclear issue is the improvement in relations between North Korea and the United States, on the one hand, and between North Korea and Japan, on the other. But what will the impact be on relations between North and South Korea?

Most initial reactions were ones of concern—that instead of progressing along the paths of cooperation and harmony, relations between the two countries will become more competitive. Further, if North Korea establishes diplomatic relations with the United States and Japan, there is a chance that such recognition, premised on there being two distinct nations on the Korean peninsula, would translate to a diplomatic policy on the part of Japan and the United States that in effect treated both North and South Korea equally.

If this were to be the case, the future relationship between North and South could not be characterized as one between people of the same ethnic group, but rather as "international relations" between two countries caught up in the political and economic interests of East Asia's four major powers—the United States, Russia, China, and Japan. Consequently, the odds that the North and South would be able to determine the destiny of the peninsula would be further reduced.

In any case, it is undeniable that in the short run, US relaxation of economic sanctions against the North and Japanese transfusion of "reparations" would strengthen the North Korean economy. In the long run, reunification of North and South would be delayed, and the South might find itself engaged in fierce diplomatic competition with the major powers in the region. Even if concrete economic cooperation were to be established with the North, South Korea would likely be deliberately excluded from this process, first by Japan and the nations of the West.

The North may be attempting to engender a strategy whereby it encourages competition between Western and Korean sources of capital in the hopes of reaping the greatest material gain. South Korea simply cannot exclude the possibility that increased economic exchange between North Korea and the West, and especially with Japan, will diminish the need for economic cooperation between North and South.

Yet, there are positive aspects. An improvement of US and Japanese relations with North Korea, accompanied by complete cross-recognition among the four major powers, could make rocky international relations in East Asia that much more secure. This security dynamic would represent a fundamental change in the region that could accelerate North Korea's opening and thus strengthen the security of the whole peninsula.

But South Korea must be cautious. Cross-recognition would increase the influence of the four major powers on reunification of the peninsula.

Chinese and Russian Policies Toward the Peninsula

The nuclear accord and the consequent improvement in US–North Korean relations has sparked increased interest in China and Russia, and there are some indications of actual moves by those countries to strengthen relations with North Korea. Thus, resolution of the North Korean nuclear issue appears to be a precursor to the reshuffling of the power structure in East Asia.

China's intentions were well expressed by Prime Minister Li Peng at a 4 November 1994 press conference held at the conclusion of his historic visit to South Korea. After contending that "China has deep interests in peace and stability in the East Asian region including the Korean peninsula," Li proposed that "the two Koreas and other related parties take part in the process of setting up a peace system to replace the armistice agreement that halted the 1950–53 Korean War" (*Korea Times*, 5 November 1994). The statement hints that China's position would be to craft a "two plus two plan;" that is, in any new arrangement regarding North and South Korea, the United States and China would both participate.

With this formulation, China appears to be paving the way toward including both South Korea, which insists as a matter of principle on being a party to these discussions, and North Korea, which intends to focus on its agreement with the United States, to the exclusion of South Korea. Further, China indicates its intention to take a leading role in the East Asian realignment that is expected following recognition by the four major powers of North and South Korea.

On 1 September 1994 China announced the recall of its representatives to the Military Armistice Commission. This action can be interpreted as a strategic step toward strengthening the North's position in its negotiations for a peace agreement with the United States, ultimately leading to the withdrawal of US forces from the peninsula and curbing the increase in US influence on the peninsula. This move also suggests that, even after the death of Kim Il Sung, Chinese–North Korean military and security cooperation will continue. China has evidently decided that in the interest of securing its own socialist system it will support Kim Jung Il's system and the security of North Korea as a whole, thus continuing to include North Korea in its own sphere of influence. In this vein, an established China specialist has argued:

> Beijing seems determined enough not to have another socialist regime collapsing on its vital northern strategic *cordons sanitaire*, nor chaos nor war, with the ominous implications that would have for its domestic and regional stability (including a flood of refugees joining its already uncontrollable floating population within its porous borders). . . . To abandon Pyongyang is to lose whatever leverage Beijing may still have on the politics of divided Korea, or to reduce it to the level Russia has today, which is very marginal. (Samuel S. Kim 1994, 722–23)

What then is Russia's position? Russia established diplomatic relations with South Korea in 1990 in expectation of economic support from South Korea. Russia thus demonstrated a tilt toward the South that invited the North's protests and anger. But it has been disappointed in its hopes of aid. At least partly to provoke South Korea, Russia has been pursuing a diplomatic policy that would treat North and South equally. In April 1994, when international sanctions were seriously discussed at the UN Security Council, the Yeltsin government declared that Russia would carry out its obligations under the 1961 mutual security treaty, providing military backing to North Korea if the North were attacked without provocation. At the same time, it promoted a multilateral conference involving China, Japan, Russia, the United States, the two Koreas, the United Nations, and the IAEA to resolve the issue (*International Herald Tribune*, 10 April 1994, 9). In June 1994, when the nuclear issue heated up again, Yeltsin revived the eight-power conference proposal, or an eight-power consultative body as an alternative, to provide a cooling-off period. As one observer aptly pointed out:

> Being left out of China's bilateral approach and marginalized by US hegemonic sanctions diplomatically, Russia was thus attempting to get back into the game.

... Such Russian readiness to enter the multidimensional nuclear shell game on the Korean peninsula as a great power stems not only from Russia's traditional role as a geostrategic balancer on the Korean Peninsula along with China and Japan, but also the realization that the Russians made the cardinal strategic mistake of putting all their eggs into the South Korean basket at the expense of their leverage in Pyongyang." (Samuel S. Kim 1994, 724 and 725)

Despite its efforts to get back into the Korean game, in the resolution of the nuclear issue Russia has felt a great deal of alienation, especially in the selection of the type of light-water reactor to be installed in the North. Russia had fervently hoped that its own type of light-water reactor would be chosen to replace North Korea's current model. On 25 January 1995, Deputy Foreign Minister Alexander Panov told the ITAR-Tass news agency: "Russia wants a major role in reforming North Korea's nuclear program and will not agree to be a junior brother in an international consortium being set up to create a new program" (*Korea Times*, 26 January 1995). For South Korea, it is urgent both that Russia's feelings be soothed and that it find a way to build on its relations with the former Soviet Union.

Prospects for North-South Dialogue

The Kim Jung Il regime must find a solution to its economic problems within the structural limitations of its present circumstances. Having begun to normalize relations with the United States and perhaps also with Japan on the strength of the nuclear issue, Kim now must stabilize his regime and his own authority.

On the domestic front, Kim Jung Il must curb reform as much as possible to ensure the continuation of a regime that recognizes him as its solitary leader. Yet it also appears that Kim will attempt various policies such as the development of "tourist complexes" as well as the securing of, and additional construction at North Korea's "free economic and trade zones."

On the international front, North Korea will seek further normalization of relations. In the case of the United States, liaison offices are to open, and with Japan, a trade representative's office. North Korea thus should be able to overcome its diplomatic isolation and its economic difficulties at the same time. To no small extent, this would help ensure the stability of the North Korean regime—hence its do-or-die efforts at normalization. In this post–Cold War era, it is likely that the United States and Japan will want to pursue policies that include North Korea in a new regional and world order.

Yet North Korea's policies will retain much of their Cold War character. It will avoid comparisons of the two systems based on the numbers—economic and other data—and continue to emphasize the legitimacy of its role as the standard bearer of Korean nationalism while the South has degenerated into "a colony of international capitalism." In other words, the battle of ideologies and mind games will continue.

Consequently, it is likely that any resumption of North-South dialogue will be a matter of form only, in order to facilitate improved relations with the United States and Japan. After its withdrawal from the NPT on 12 March 1993, the North has deftly employed its strategy of direct negotiations with the United States as its solution to Korean peninsula problem. This means "talks *primarily* with the United States" and "*secondarily* talks with South Korea."

North Korea's first overture for inter-Korean dialogue since the death of Kim Il Sung, made on 24 January 1995, should be read in this context. North Korea did propose a dialogue with the South, not seeking government-to-government contact but rather a convening of a "grand national conference" of the "political parties, factions, and compatriots from all walks of life," including those residing overseas but excluding government authorities. South Korea portrayed the conference as "a mass rally" with little substance and counterproposed official meetings at the vice ministerial level. North Korea immediately rejected this proposal (*Korea Times*, 26, 27, and 28 January 1995). What was its motivation? The answer is, North Korea proposed the national congress because it must engage in inter-Korean dialogue under the agreed framework in Geneva. Regardless of the results of its overture, the North could claim it had fulfilled its obligations.

South Korea's Diplomatic and Reunification Policy: A Few Guidelines

In light of the changes in political climate following the resolution of the US–North Korean nuclear accord, what direction should South Korea follow in constructing diplomatic and reunification policies?

After the Geneva accord, one could sum up the political climate on the peninsula as one in which the North began a fundamental effort to improve relations between itself and the United States as well as Japan. China and Russia, in an effort to buck this trend, will continue to interfere in matters affecting the Korean peninsula. Thus, there will be both positive and negative aspects to the change in political climate on the peninsula. On the plus side, the security of the peninsula should become a less pressing concern, and North Korea's opening should accelerate. On the negative side, one can expect North-South diplomatic competition and conflict between the four major regional powers.

In order to make use of the positive aspects and minimize the effects of the negative, South Korea must avoid taking the critical, reactive stance that has characterized its policies and public statements since the accord was signed and must form a much more positive attitude toward dialogue with the North. Because North Korea attaches greater importance to its relations with the United States and Japan and consequently puts its discussion with South Korea on the back burner, the South must seek the initiative. On another front, the South must alter its view of the four major powers as one entity—a far too simplistic stance—to one that evaluates each nation as an individual entity.

With improvements in US-North Korean relations, the armistice agreement as well as the removal of US forces from Korea will again become pertinent. It is inevitable that US-South Korean relations must undergo an overhaul. At the same time, South Korea is unable to exercise much influence over Japan's overtures to North Korea.

In relations with Russia and China, South Korea must also overcome a *Nordpolitik* of old based on the containment of North Korea. The South needs to formulate new relationships built on mutual interests, and its government must be prepared to craft measures to support such developments.

With the signing of the Geneva accord, the most pressing South Korean concern is the transition from a relationship with the North carried out under the rubric of an armistice commission to a peacetime system. After proposing the resolution of the peace agreement with the United States, on 28 April 1994 North Korea's Ministry of Foreign Affairs issued a statement that North Korea was withdrawing its representative to the armistice commission. China followed suit. In effect, the Military Armistice Commission has become an organization in name only. This became even more evident when North Korea forced the United States to ignore the Military Armistice Commission in negotiations surrounding the December 1994 downing of an American helicopter in North Korean airspace. As discussed above, North Korea succeeded in making a high-ranking US government official visit Pyongyang and hold meetings with North Korean authorities.

Subsequently, the South Korean government has explored ways to transform its diplomatic strategy—from one that emphasizes pressuring the North into a "postnuclear" diplomacy to one that emphasizes creating a peacetime framework on the peninsula. In executing such a policy, several points should be considered.

Transforming an existing armistice-based system to a peacetime system involves building trust, concluding a peace agreement, and securing the peace. A logical first step into this process must be the sincere execution of, and willingness to abide by, the Joint Declaration on the Denuclearization of the Korean Peninsula of 13 December 1991, and the Basic Agreement on Reconciliation, Non-Aggression, Exchanges and Cooperation of 31 December 1991, which provided the basic framework for the parties to conclude an agreement. These two agreements, which became effective in February 1992, are still valid.

In particular, until the armistice agreement is transformed into a peace agreement, the military armistice agreement concluded in July 1953 must be strictly adhered to. In order to make that possible, the following measures must be implemented:

- No steps should be taken that could be construed as peremptory changes to the system put in place by the military armistice agreement.
- The functions of the Military Armistice Commission must return to normal.
- The activities of Poland, the "communist representative" on the Neutral Nations Supervisory Commission, must be resumed and its continued operations and activities must be guaranteed.

The South Korean government, while continuing to adhere to these principles, should also convene a Joint Commission on North-South Cooperation, as stipulated in the Basic Agreement of 1991. Specifically, this forum should investigate measures that could be taken to revise and supplement the basic agreement and to adopt the Korean Peninsula Peace Declaration and appendices.

After the basic framework for a peacetime system has been laid, an international guarantee system should be implemented to ensure its integrity. One way to craft this international guarantee would be through "two plus four" talks—that is, North and South as well as the four major powers. A multinational security agreement system in East Asia would provide a framework for discussions on guaranteeing a peacetime system on the Korean peninsula and ensuring comprehensive security cooperation in East Asia.

Serious obstacles to the resumption of talks between North and South Korea remain. With the death of Kim Il Sung, the North-South summit talks to have been held on 25 July 1994 in Pyongyang were canceled. Since then, the formal transfer of power has been delayed, and the emphasis since the elder Kim's death has been placed on improved relations with the United States. In short, antipathy toward the South has prevailed, to the detriment of continued North-South talks.

However, the nuclear accord stipulated that talks be resumed with the South. This as much as anything else provides an opportunity for actively promoting the resumption of North-South dialogue.

South Korea would prefer that talks by the Joint Commission on Nuclear Non-Proliferation, as stipulated in the Denuclearization of the Korean Peninsula Agreement, be reconvened and that mutual inspections and discussion on the peaceful use of nuclear energy be undertaken. However, it is inevitable that more realistic plans will be discussed—for example, support for the construction of a light-water reactor and financial support for alternative energy sources. South Korea should use this opportunity to convene a Joint Economic Commission or a working-level Energy Development Agreement meeting in order to discuss technical and financial cooperation.

Further, if South Korea is really interested in resuming talks with North Korea, there are a few steps it could take to create a climate conducive to dialogue. First, the South should avoid making inflammatory remarks about the North. Second, as the North continues to insist on direct talks with the United States on concluding a peace agreement, the South should wage its offensive on a different level: exploring proposals for armament reduction talks to build trust on military issues and for talks on reuniting separated families and repatriating those imprisoned in the North that wish to be returned to the South.

The South should make every effort to research how to use the window of opportunity that should open after North Korea completes its formal transfer of power. In particular, when the North reaches the final stages of its transfer of power, the South should consider ways in which to conduct a summit with the North's new leader to ascertain the new government's policy directions and discuss proposals for improving North-South relations. Convening a North-South summit meeting early in the new North Korean administration's term might be an advantageous method for building trust between the two sides. While there are already certain agreed-upon principles and procedures still in effect, circumstances have changed; thus the place, time, and order of the opening of such a summit meeting must unavoidably be decided after new discussion.

The South once linked resolution of the nuclear problem to economic cooperation, believing that the nuclear agreement must establish the basic principles governing any subsequent agreements on other issues. But with the conclusion of the US–North Korean nuclear accord, the South has been freed from this linkage doctrine. As a result, the South Korean government in December 1994 officially lifted the ban on investments by South Korean businessmen in the North. Large firms including the Daewoo Group, the Ssangyong group, and the Samsung group have already sent investment teams to the North.

The US decision to relax restrictions on trade and investment in North Korea is likely a harbinger of future expansion of economic cooperation between North Korea and the United States. As the North continues along the path set in the nuclear accord, the South should permit its business leaders to visit North Korea more freely, dispatch South Korean technicians to the North, and allow direct trade and investment by its entrepreneurs.

Other exchanges, through sports events or academic conferences and meetings, for example, could be pursued as well. A potentially important point of contact may be the Korean Energy Development Organization (KEDO), newly formed within the framework of the Geneva accord. Under its aegis, North and South Korean engineers, technicians, and energy experts, faced with the task of building light-water reactors, could begin practical discussions. Letting unofficial, private-sector activity expand for perhaps six to ninth months might make both sides more comfortable dealing with each other and could provide an opening for official dialogue at the prime ministerial or summit level (Manning 1995).

A final point is that there will never be peace on the Korean peninsula until there is reduction in conventional arms. That process can only come about through North-South dialogue. In this context, any discussions on replacing the armistice agreement with a peace treaty or an alternative must include South Korea as a key party to the negotiations, and it must be a signatory to any replacement agreement.

References

Kim, Hong-nack. 1994. "Japan's North Korea Policy in the Post–Cold War Era." *Korea & World Affairs* 18, no. 4 (Winter): 694.

Kim, Samuel S. 1994. "Chinese and Russian Perspectives and Policies toward the Korean Reunification Issue." *Korea & World Affairs* 18, no. 4 (Winter): 722–23.

Manning, Robert A. 1995. "1995 Will Be Key to Shaping Fate of Korea," *Korea Times* (12 January).

3

Economic Integration on the Korean Peninsula: Effects and Implications

YOUNG-SUN LEE

The year 1995 marks the 50th anniversary of independence for the Korean peninsula. However, these years were also a period of painful separation. Today, in the 50th year of division, the spirit of change is in the air. Talks between North Korea and the United States have brought the nuclear issue under control, and fears of confusion in North Korea over Kim Il Sung's death hindering peace efforts on the Korean peninsula have subsided. Nevertheless, the inherent instability within North Korea, coupled with the demise of the Cold War and Kim Il Sung, promises further changes.

As in the former socialist countries in Eastern Europe, the chief cause of instability in North Korea is economic difficulties: a Stalinist, autocratic economic system coupled with the inefficiencies of a closed economy and the dismantling of the cooperative system among socialist countries. Kim Jung Il faces the huge task of overcoming economic hardships while maintaining the socialist system in his country.

The possibilities of change in North Korea will continue to have far-reaching effects on the future of the South, thus posing a significant challenge to South Korea's government. Continued high economic growth in the South depends on how the situation progresses in the North and on economic cooperation between the two sides. Therefore, the latest developments in economic exchange and cooperation between South and North Korea are of utmost importance for peace and prosperity on the peninsula.

Young-Sun Lee is professor of economics at Yonsei University in Seoul.

This chapter examines the economic realities in North Korea and seeks to shed light on the possibilities for reform. It then analyzes the effects of unification in terms of costs and benefits and looks into issues relating to economic integration on the Korean peninsula.

North Korea's Economic Situation and the Possibility of Reform

Macroeconomic Indicators

It is not easy to obtain or derive the macroeconomic indicators needed to reveal the state of economic difficulty in the North. GNP figures are not publicly reported by the North Korean government, and even if they were available, they would undoubtedly be misleading.[1] In an effort to overcome this problem, the Bank of Korea has for the past couple of years resorted to an indirect method for calculating the North's GNP figures. Although it remains somewhat questionable as to whether the data truly reflect economic conditions in the North, they are all that is available, and they are quite reliable indicators of the overall direction of the economy in the North.

Table 1 compares key economic indicators of North Korea to those of the South. Nominal GNP figures for 1993 reveal North Korea's economy to be one-sixteenth the size of the South's. With half the South's population, North Korea has a per capita GNP that is one-eighth that of the South. This difference between the two Koreas, which is far greater than that between the two German nations before reunification, indicates that the burden South Korea must bear after reunification will be relatively greater than that of West Germany.[2]

Clearly, the North's economic system is to blame for the large difference in per capita income between the two Koreas. When Korea was liberated from Japanese rule, economic conditions were more favorable for the North because the Japanese had concentrated industrial facilities there because of the region's abundant deposits of raw materials and had left the South a largely agricultural region. Furthermore, as with other socialist countries, North Korea met with considerable success at the initial stages of implementing the Stalinist system. Japanese rule left the overpopulated South foundering in the quagmire of absolute

---

1. In 1988, North Korea reported its per capita GNP as $3,008. But this figure reflects only the living standard of those living in Pyongyang. Living standards in the rural regions are far below that of Pyongyang.

2. Per capita income and population for East Germany before reunification were one-half and one-quarter that of West Germany, respectively.

Table 1   North and South Korea: macroeconomic indicators, 1990–93

Indicator	North Korea (A)				South Korea (B)				(B/A)
	1990	1991	1992	1993	1990	1991	1992	1993	1993
Nominal GNP (billions of dollars)	23.7	22.9	21.1	20.5	255.8	281.7	294.5	328.7	16.0
Per capita GNP (dollars)		1,038	943	904		6,518	6,749	7,466	8.3
Growth rate (percent)	−3.7	−5.2	−7.6	−4.3	9.2	8.4	5.0	5.6	
Population (thousands)		22,028	22,336	22,645		43,268	43,663	44,056	1.9
Trade (billions of dollars)		2.72	2.66	2.64		153.4	158.4	166.0	62.9
Exports (billions of dollars)		1.01	1.02	1.02		71.87	76.63	82.24	80.6
Imports (billions of dollars)		1.71	1.64	1.62		81.52	81.78	83.8	51.7
Foreign debt (billions of dollars)		9.28	9.72	10.32		39.13	42.82	44.08	4.3
Foreign debt as a share of GNP		40.5	46.0	50.3		13.9	14.5	13.4	

Sources: Bank of Korea, 1994, *Annual Economic Statistics,* and *Report on Estimation of North Korean GNP,* Seoul.

poverty, a situation exacerbated by the Korean War. With an abundant supply of natural resources, fewer people, and an initially effective economic system armed with revolutionary ideology, per capita GNP in North Korea surpassed that of the South until the 1970s, when South Korea's economy began to take off. But inefficiency, a lack of incentives, a lack of new technological inputs due to the closed nature of the economy, and aging, deteriorating industrial facilities partially destroyed during the war brought North Korean economic growth to a standstill. Meanwhile, the South adopted an outward-looking economic development strategy that led to rapid economic growth and a widening gap in per capita GNP on the peninsula.

While North Korea is concerned that it is falling further and further behind the South, the more immediate concern is its current negative growth rate. As can be seen from table 1, the North Korea economy declined from 1991 to 1993. Figures for 1994 have not been released, but no one believes that the trend has been reversed. Since the end of the 1980s, the size of North Korea's economy has decreased by 30 percent. Regardless of how strongly the North Korean government believes in the moral superiority of its system, it can no longer guarantee acceptable living standards for its people in the face of such significant economic decline. Thus, speculations of brewing political instability cannot be unfounded.

Table 2   North Korea: trade volume, 1987–92
(millions of dollars)

Year	Exports	Imports	Balance
1987	1,469	−2,568	−1,099
1988	1,822	−3,199	−1,377
1989	1,686	−2,905	−1,219
1990	1,857	−2,930	−1,073
1991[a]	1,400	−2,310	−910
1992[a]	920	−1,550	−630

a. These numbers may be inconsistent with other numbers (including those in table 1) because of differences in sources.

Source: Economist Intelligence Unit, 1994, Country Report: South Korea and North Korea.

With the exception of China, other socialist countries also experienced negative economic growth rates in the 1990s. The negative growth rates recorded by Eastern European countries reflect the costs of readjustment necessary for structural change. In the case of North Korea, other factors explain its economic decline. First, it received extensive economic aid from the former Soviet Union. Similarly, prior to China's open-door policy and marketization, it was able to alleviate its food and energy shortages through a compensatory trade channel. However, the breakup of the Soviet Union brought economic aid to a halt, and with the sweeping economic changes in China taking place, the Chinese government is officially asking for hard-currency payments for its goods. Since North Korea has a short supply of foreign currency, such demands are causing difficulties for them.

The foreign trade volume figures shown in table 2 differ from those in table 1. Because the government of North Korea releases no such figures, those of both tables have been estimated using varying sources and exchange rates, thus accounting for the difference in figures. The Bank of Korea estimates that the North's trade volume remained at a standstill throughout the early 1990s. The Economic Intelligence Unit, on the other hand, claims that it has decreased markedly over the same period. In any case, trade is stagnant, causing food and energy shortages and impeding economic growth.

In accordance with its self-reliance principle, North Korea imports only goods of utmost need and exports for the sole purpose of earning foreign currency to service its imports. However, a domestic manufacturing system that is indifferent to foreign market conditions led to a decrease in export volume, and the trade balance fell into the red, contributing to a foreign debt level of $10 billion in 1993. In absolute figures, South Korean foreign debt is higher, at $44 billion, but once foreign assets are accounted for, the net foreign debt falls to roughly $10 billion. Even so, the South Korean debt is less significant because the country's

Table 3   North Korea: production of key industrial sectors, 1989–93

Industry	Unit	1989	1990	1991	1992	1993
Energy						
Coal	Million tons	35.08	33.15	31.00	29.20	27.10
Electricity	Billion kw hrs	29.37	27.74	26.30	24.70	22.10
Crude oil imports	Million tons	2.72	2.52	1.89	1.52	1.36
Agriculture						
Grain	Million tons	4.58	4.02	4.43	4.27	3.88
Rice	Million tons	2.16	1.46	1.64	1.63	1.32
Marine products	Million tons	2.19	1.45	1.20	1.14	1.09
Mining						
Iron ore	Million tons	9.00	8.43	8.17	5.75	4.76
Nonferrous metal	Million tons	0.25	0.24	0.23	0.18	0.16
Heavy industries and petrochemicals						
Automobiles	1,000 cars	15	13	12	10	10
Shipbuilding	1,000 G/T	23	38	40	55	51
Steel	1,000 tons	3,414	3,364	3,168	1,793	1,860
Cement	1,000 tons	5,100	6,130	5,169	4,747	3,980
Fertilizer	1,000 tons	1,658	1,586	1,435	1,385	1,609
Light industries						
Weaving	Million m	210	200	210	170	190
Textiles	1,000 tons	44	50	54	42	53

Source: Hansei Policy Institute, 1994, *North Korean Economy Monthly* (December): 37–38.

annual export volume is close to $100 billion. Total foreign debt for the North, on the other hand, is 10 times that of its annual export volume.

Declines in production and socioeconomic conditions are reflected in the real output changes of major sectors. Table 3 shows the quantity of physical units produced in these sectors rather than the monetary value of output.

The table shows that production in the energy sector has been steadily declining since 1989. Coal production for 1993 stopped at 27.1 million tons, 23 percent less than in 1989. Generated electric power dropped 25 percent within the same period, recording a mere 22.1 billion kilowatt hours in 1993. Furthermore, imports of crude petroleum decreased by half, falling to 1.36 million tons in 1993.

Statistics for food production in North Korea reveal the severity of the food shortage problem. Rice production for 1993 fell roughly 40 percent as compared with 1989, recording 1.32 million tons, and overall cereal production fell by 15 percent within the same period, to a mere 3.88 million tons. Such a decline in agricultural production can be attributed to the fall in labor productivity due to the absence of incentives, the destruction of arable land due to blights and other harmful insects, and the inability to produce or import the necessary fertilizers and chemicals. The Economist Intelligence Unit estimates that in 1993 demand for foodstuffs came to 6.85 million tons, but total supply fell short by 2.34

million tons (EIU 1993). Marine products production in 1993 fell to half that of 1989.

The decline in the North Korean economy is also evident in the slow-down of industrial manufacturing. Insufficient supply of energy has led to a production decline in the automobile, steel, cement, textile, and other light industries.

Official reports of the North Korean government confirm this decline. At the end of 1993, the North Korean government admitted that it could no longer carry out its third seven-year plan. This acknowledgment of failure in economic planning, never seen before, clearly reveals the gravity of the situation. Furthermore, since 1993 the North Korean government has passed budgets with growth rates much lower than those of previous years. Until 1992, 6 percent increases in expenditure and revenue were appropriated on average. In 1993 this fell to 2 to 3 percent and has remained at that level.

Another hardship on the North's economy is the drastic decrease in remittances by Chochongryun (an association of Korean residents in Japan supporting North Korea). An information source in Japan states that until recently, Chochongryun had sent an annual ¥80 billion (about $747 million) in currency and produce to North Korea. These remittances were instrumental in balancing North Korea's current account. However, the recent trend of stagnation in the Japanese economy, along with international pressures for sanctions tied to the nuclear proliferation issue, has caused remittances to fall, aggravating the situation for North Korea.

The ongoing economic hardships and food shortages have led many to question the stability of the current political structure in North Korea. Although there have been unofficial reports of unrest, in particular the looting of foodstuffs, it cannot be officially confirmed. Furthermore, stability may have returned since the death of Kim Il Sung. Whatever the case may be, economic hardship and the overall low standard of living of the North is pressuring those in power to make changes.

Possibilities for Economic Reform and Opening

How will the North Korean government face the steadily increasing need for change and the opening of the economy? The leadership must first realize the need for openness and the need to rely on market principles. They have to see that the backwardness of the economy can be attributed to centralized economic planning and the closed nature of the system. The characteristics of the North Korean political system necessitate that change begin at the top and be transferred down the ladder. However, the question remains whether the privileged who are in power will be willing to attempt opening, a process that could very well destabilize the current political order. North Korea will undoubtedly be wary of happenings similar to the Tiananmen Square incident in China during its opening phase of economic reform. North Korea is also well aware that despite this event, market principles have taken hold and rapid economic progress has occurred under the old autocratic political system in China. However, North Korea's caution stems in part from a fear of possible moral confusion of the populace and the subsequent political instability that could arise. To reap the benefits of opening and market principles, while minimizing political risk, the North Korean government has chosen the relatively sparsely populated and somewhat isolated Najin-Sunbong region as an economic free trade zone. Whether or not changes similar to those that occurred in China take place in North Korea depends on the stability of the North Korean government.

This political stability in turn rests on improvements in North Korean living standards. Paradoxically, the economic reforms North Korea needs to ensure long-term political stability could also result in political instability. The current government cannot be confident that reforms will not undermine its legitimacy. Therefore, it strengthened its control through a championing of moral values set forth by the late Kim Il Sung. Economic considerations are second on the agenda.

When the government acknowledged the failure of its third seven-year plan, it declared the next two to three years as a "buffer period for the construction of socialism." The strategy is directed toward alleviating economic hardships by focusing on agriculture, light industries, and trade. This drive had three main goals: the elimination of food shortages through an "agriculture first" policy, the supply of daily necessities through a "light industry first" policy and the promotion of export activities for the accumulation of foreign currency, to be used in purchasing energy, through a "trade first policy." Furthermore, in order to raise living standards and establish a self-reliant economy, leading sectors such as coal, energy, and railways are being actively promoted, and changes are being carried out in the agricultural land ownership system, from the past cooperative union structure to "full people's ownership"—namely, government ownership.

Such strategies clearly indicate not only the extent of North Korean economic difficulties, they also delineate the government's policy stance. Despite past failures of collectivization, as evidenced by the *sovkhoz* system in Russia and the "people's corporation" in China, North Korea insists on returning to this system because they attribute its past failures to a lack of revolutionary ideology among the peasantry and a lack of technology in the agricultural sector. By nationalizing the cooperative farms, North Korea has proclaimed the continuity of what it calls "our style of socialism." But the reshuffling of the agricultural organization serves to strengthen internal control and reveals the all-too-narrow limits of economic reform.

In its trade-first policy the government stresses a slogan for quality improvement, "clean finishing and packaging," which is concerned with production of exportable goods through Najin-Sunbong. However, North Korea's efforts to promote economic cooperation with the United States, Japan, and countries of Southeast Asia are merely a part of its strategy to maintain the political and economic system. The degree of openness that Najin-Sunbong represents cannot be understood as an effort to reform the system but can only be viewed as an effort at retaining it.

Would it really be possible for North Korea to experience the Chinese style of reform? Many scholars are skeptical. They doubt that North Korea, which has indoctrinated its people in the *juche* ideology, could readily introduce a market system and open its economy. The possibility for political destabilization is the main reason for their skepticism. Furthermore, it is doubtful that bureaucrats accustomed to a centralized administrative system could accept the dispersion of authority and the political liberalization that would follow economic liberalization. Nonetheless, many observers believe that reform is inevitable because of pressures arising from North Korea's economic difficulties. They cite as evidence the various efforts being made to induce foreign firms, including South Korean firms, to invest in Najin-Sunbong. It may be that looming economic imperatives coupled with attendant political risks will lead North Korea to reform the economy gradually. It is also conceivable that a new faction could use the need for economic development as an excuse for seizing power.

North-South Economic Integration: Its Costs and Benefits

North-South political and economic reunification has been Koreans' cherished desire ever since the division of the peninsula. With the end of the Cold War, realizing of this wish seems more possible than ever. However, the vestiges of the Cold War are still lingering on the peninsula, and the North Korean government, which is holding fast to its socialist system, is still very much in power. Under such circumstances, is reunification indeed a possibility?

North-South reunification depends on the North. It is true that South Koreans have not reached consensus on the extent of the socioeconomic burden they are willing to shoulder and that they have not made preparations for reunification. But as the predominant economic power and with its political stability, South Korea will be able to rise to the occasion, just as West Germany was when it came time to reunify Germany. Furthermore, most citizens of South Korea want reunification. The issue is whether North Korea is willing to make the necessary adjustments.

The continuity of the system in North Korea and the reunification process will be greatly influenced by the method employed to pursue these two goals. An interesting development since the death of Kim Il Sung is that the prospects for changing the North Korean system have heightened. A survey of Korean and non-Korean experts on the Korean peninsula showed most thought before Kim Il Sung's death this event would portend the end of the status quo and that rapid progress toward reunification would take place before the year 2000. Yet after witnessing a peaceful and legitimate transfer of power, more and more experts are predicting that the current system will continue for a long time. In a survey of 50 experts after Kim Il Sung's death, the majority of respondents felt that Kim Jung Il would maintain the current political structure while carrying out closely monitored economic development plans (Lee 1995). This did not necessarily mean that the majority also believed that North Korea would achieve political stability and economic development.

According to the survey, North Korea faces three obstacles. In fact, it may have surmounted the first—namely, the restoration of political stability following the death of Kim Il Sung. Though it may still be a little early to conclude that the transition of power has been completed, it appears that political stability has to date prevailed, despite the forecasts.

The second hurdle is the current economic difficulties. North Korea must reform its economy, yet most experts do not believe North Korea can do so. The prevailing opinion is that the North will attempt economic development through changes in the power structure that will eventually lead to the system's collapse, although this will not occur overnight. North Korea's lack of success in economic reform will in turn delay reunification.

The third hurdle North Korea will face is democratization or pluralism. If the North were to achieve steady economic growth and build a political system based upon consensus of the governed, North and South could coexist and eventually be reunited by general consent. Many experts, including a number of Chinese academicians, believe that this is the most reasonable path, and they thus predict a protracted period of coexistence. Whether North Korea actually overcomes these obstacles is beyond the scope of this chapter. The important point is that regardless of whether it occurs through the breakup of the North Korean system or through general consensus, reunification will be possible only after a considerable time span.

Once it occurs, Korean reunification may be very different from German reunification, which took place with the fall of socialism and changes in Soviet policy toward East Germany. The Korean case differs in that North Korea has been more independent of its neighboring socialist countries than was East Germany, so that neither China's nor Russia's changed policy toward North Korea will influence it very much. Furthermore, the Korean War produced feelings of animosity between the two Korean sides that the Germanys did not experience. East and West Germany exchanged goods, people, and information for an extended period before reunification. Such exchanges have not been possible between the Koreans. But they are necessary. It is unreasonable to think that North Koreans would readily be assimilated into South Korea simply because of the economic hardships they face, or that social unrest would automatically lead to reunification. In any case, according to the survey mentioned previously, the possibility of a people's revolt in North Korea before the year 2000 is minimal.

If South Koreans are sincere in their wish for reunification, how should they prepare themselves? South Korea can formulate policies to influence North Korea's choices. Economic aid and cooperation may prop up the current power structure in the short run. In the long run, though, such aid will promote change and reduce the overall costs of reunification.

With the reunification of Germany and the possibility that something similar may occur on the Korean peninsula, many people are now discussing unification costs. However, the debate has been fraught with confusion due to inconsistent use of terms and differing assumptions.

In particular, clarification of the definitions for "unification" and "costs" are in order. Generally, the word cost refers to two main concepts. Accounting cost is used for general purposes, and the concept of opportunity cost is used for economic purposes. Almost all of the figures released to date on unification costs refer solely to accounting costs. They include items such as a postreunification guarantee of livelihood and job training for the North Koreans, the replacement of backward industrial facilities of the North, infrastructural investment, and provision of other public facilities and services. Estimates of these unification costs have shown large disparities, ranging from $1.3 trillion by Professor Shin Chang Min to $85.9 billion by the Korea Development Institute (Park 1994, 63–77). Differing assumptions of the levels of social support, industrial spending, and infrastructure investment that South Koreans will be willing to make account for these disparities. Thus, the degree of economic aid that will be extended to the North must be made clear before these estimates can be reconciled. Once this is done, the accounting cost measure may be used as a basic reference for appropriating financial resources. However, accounting costs will only illuminate the financial cost structure of the aid program and will provide no information on public welfare losses and benefits.

The "opportunity cost" concept, however, can offer before- and after-comparisons of public welfare data thus providing information for policymakers. Using a scenario approach, I have estimated the degree of sacrifice required of South Koreans in terms of income opportunity and the income benefit North Koreans could reap (Lee 1994, 207–22). I took reunification to mean the economic integration of the peninsula—that is, the same per capita output applies to the people of both sides. In other words, through economic integration the level of per capita output on the peninsula will be standardized.

The form of reunification assumed here is one that can only be achieved through the long and gradual efforts of both sides. The South will transfer a portion of its GNP (the portion attributed to the growth rate) to the North, where it will be used solely for investments.[3] The North will also extend economic reform in order to increase its efficiency, and in the year economic integration occurs, a full-fledged market system should be adopted.

Without any efforts for reunification, the South and the North are assumed to grow at rates of 6.75 percent and 4.5 percent, respectively. Once efforts for reunification are under way, transfer payments will reduce the growth rate of the South to 6.3 percent, and the annual growth rate of the North will consequently rise to over 10 percent during the initial stages and steadily decline to a level equal to that of the South. The production-investment relationship was developed using a simple marginal output-capital ratio to develop the Harrod-Domar growth model. South Korean reunification costs attributable to sacrificed income opportunity are shown as the difference between GNP when there is no reunification and GNP when efforts for reunification are made, plus transfer payments to North Korea, minus the decrease in military expenditure. On the other hand, the benefit to North Korea is the difference between GNP when efforts for reunification are made and GNP when efforts are not made. This method of calculation continues until per capita output for the two sides becomes equal and total reunification costs and reunification benefits are calculated. A discount rate of 10 percent is applied in order to convert these sums to present value.

Following these assumptions, reunification costs and benefits were calculated with 1990 as the base year. The North and South require 42 years to achieve equivalent per capita GNP, and during this time the South needs to supply the North with $330 billion, and the people of the South will experience a loss of $841 billion in income opportunity. This sum is 2.8 times the size of South Korea's GNP of $238 billion in

---

3. The North Korean government regards as investment all the budgeted funds necessary for equipment and construction in the expansion of production, such as basic construction funds, operational funds for primary and intermediate materials, price subsidies for food and necessities, aid to self-supported factories, aid to farms, funds for development of science and technology, funds for projects for urban and rural administration, and funds for foreign economic projects. Although most of these funds could increase the capital stock for future production, some of them cannot be regarded as investment. Therefore, it is logical for the incremental output/capital ratio to be lower in the North than in the South.

1990 and is equivalent to a sacrifice of $19,500 per person in the South based on a 1990 present value. On the other hand, the people of the North receive an additional $2.44 trillion in output. Needless to say, the benefits North Koreans reap far outweigh that which the South Koreans incur. If this were not the case, efforts for reunification could not be justified. In fact, if economies of scale were included in this calculation, the figure for the gains would increase even more.

An evaluation of economic integration cannot be made only through a comparison of the costs and gains of reunification. The political issue of how the gains will be divided remains. In the previous calculations, the South Koreans supply a fixed amount of capital to the North without any form of compensation until the per capita GNP gap is closed. The income generated in this fashion is earned solely by the people of the North. Under such circumstances, it is questionable whether the people of the South would indeed be willing to undertake such a sacrifice. In order to resolve any opposition to reunification that may arise because of this sacrifice, the support package should not be transferred to the North free of charge, but rather, a portion should be transferred back. When this is done, the average production per person will be the same in both countries so that industrial activities and employment in the North will be the same as in the South. However, a portion of this value added will be used to repay the capital suppliers of the South. Therefore, equalization of income levels of the two sides will be slightly delayed.

Comparable research estimates on the costs and benefits of reunification are not available. This is because most reunification cost studies are limited to identifying the required aid expenses. The figure estimated for transfer payments in my study is comparable to the required aid expenses of other studies. Reunification costs estimated for a duration of 10 years by the KDI are $200 billion, a figure close to that which I had calculated for the same period. However, the KDI reports that during these 10 years, the per capita GNP of North Korea will reach 60 percent of South Korea's per capita GNP, whereas I have estimated this figure to be close to 30 percent.

Opportunity cost may be applied to another debate: that over whether quick or gradual reunification is less costly. Such debates occur when reunification costs are not viewed as opportunity costs but only as transfer payments. If reunification were to occur swiftly, then a large transfer payment would have to be made in a short period. However, no further transfer payments would be required after that period. Therefore, radical reunification may turn out to cost less in terms of transfer payment costs. However, swift reunification requiring a large payment today greatly reduces the opportunity for a steady flow of future income. Furthermore, when the continuous transfer payments required for gradual reunification are calculated in terms of present value, a smaller sum would result. Therefore, when opportunity costs are figured in, a gradual reunification requires less expenditure.[4]

The experience of Germany clarifies the issue. German reunification is often termed as having been radical and swift. The standardization of currency, integration of the labor market, and the adoption of private ownership rights all occurred and thus simultaneously lead one to conclude that radical economic integration indeed took place.

The cost of equalizing labor productivities in East and West Germany is as follows. East Germany's debt payment, the withdrawal costs of the Russian army, a trusteeship institution (Treuhandanstalt), East German firm management costs, and other direct costs pertaining to reunification amount to DM380 billion. Investments in infrastructure, hospitals, education, modernization of energy facilities, and the costs of narrowing the difference in living standards amount to DM640 billion. Transfer payments through social insurance institutes such as unemployment, medical, and retirement insurance amount to DM250 billion. Technological modernization for the purpose of increasing productivity of East German workers adds DM1 trillion, for a grand total of DM2.27 trillion (Kim 1993, 113). This sum is 0.95 times the GNP of West Germany for 1990. Required investment for South Korea is even greater—1.4 times its GNP for 1990.

Even if Germany is said to have achieved rapid reunification, reunification costs cannot be paid as one lump sum. If the difference in productivity and living standards were to be narrowed over 10 years, costs incurred would amount to DM227 billion per annum. This sum would be supplied by both the government and private sectors. If the private sector takes care of the private investment cost, at an annual sum of DM100 billion, the balance of DM127 billion should be provided by the government. Yet the federal government spent only DM86 billion in 1991 and DM105 billion in 1992, consuming 20 to 25 percent of the federal budget (Kim 1993, 115).

The following three methods could be implemented to lessen the government fiscal burden: increases in taxation, release of government debt, or reductions in expenditure. Fiscal demands for public goods were mostly covered by the sale of government bonds; bond revenues accounted for 68 percent in 1991 and 73 percent in 1992. Germany's volume of government bonds increased from DM70 billion in 1989 to DM140 billion in

---

4. The Korea Development Institute estimates gradual reunification costs at between $85.9 billion and $97.1 billion, and rapid reunification costs to be between $234 billion and $245 billion. Opportunity cost was not used in extrapolating these figures. Gradual reunification costs were lower than rapid reunification costs even for calculations carried out using the transfer payments concept since rapid reunification would entail almost immediate abandonment of existing industrial facilities of the North, unemployment, and other high adjustment costs.

1990, DM150 billion in 1991, and to DM200 billion in 1992 (Kim 1993, 135)[5]. The increase in the supply of government bonds caused interest rates to rise, which in turn triggered a large influx of foreign capital. Consequently, one-third of the fiscal deficit was backed by foreign purchases of German government bonds.

An increase in taxation is an effective means of supplying capital, but one that often results in political ill will and thus can be used only sparingly. Nevertheless, Kim (1993, 134) shows that this accounts for 10 to 14 percent of total revenue raised. The ratio of tax to personal income is expected to increase from the 1990 level of 41.5 percent to 45.2 percent in 1995. Germany also managed to raise revenue by reducing general expenditures by DM37 billion in 1991 and DM36 billion in 1992, accounting for 13 to 17 percent of the annual cost of reunification. Revenue from the sale of the public assets of East Germany was expected to raise some required funds. However the costs incurred for readjustment of firms and environmental cleanup proved to be larger than expected.

Private-sector investment demand should have been backed by domestic and foreign private investments. Private investment volume in East Germany amounted to DM12.8 billion in 1991, DM22.2 billion in 1992, and DM27.6 billion in 1993; the figures fell significantly behind the annual demand of DM100 billion (Kim 1993, 115) due to the sharp rise in labor costs in the East since reunification. Productivity has more or less remained constant.

As mentioned above, Korea is a different case because economic integration would occur gradually, and the unification of currency and the integration of the labor market would be set aside until the level of economic efficiency in the North rises. This will protect against problems that occurred in Germany such as the exaggerated currency value of East Germany, the subsequent rise in the level of wages, and the rapid decline of competitiveness of firms. Cost increases due to the rapid equalization of living standards may also be avoided.

Annual transfers to the North from the South ($15 billion in 1990), as assumed in my calculation of Korean unification costs, may be used for the expansion of infrastructure spending and production facilities in the North. The question of how the South Korean government intends to raise $15 billion in 1990 present value (6.3 percent of GNP) remains. Assume that the thawing of tension between the two sides allows the South to reduce military expenditures from 4 to 2 percent of its GNP. This leaves the task of providing the remaining 4.3 percent of GNP for transfers to the North. The current ratio of tax revenue to GNP is below 20 percent; this is expected to increase to a maximum of 23 percent by

---

5. The addition of regional government expenditure brings the total for 1991 to DM145 billion.

1998. Also, since this ratio is relatively lower than that of other developed countries, there is a margin of 4 to 5 percent for increasing taxes. If the demand for social welfare spending is somewhat restrained, then a total of 3 percent of GNP may be used to supply funds for reunification. The sale of government bonds cannot be relied upon since the bond market is still developing in Korea. Therefore, the remainder of the funds will need to be supplied through US and Japanese foreign direct investment in North Korea. A fraction of this amount can be expected to be supplied through American and Japanese economic aid.

Economic Exchange and Cooperation between the Two Koreas

The Importance of North-South Exchanges

Examination of the costs and benefits of a gradual process of reunification reveals that this approach costs less and yields higher gains. However, under current conditions on the peninsula, where the Cold War atmosphere still lingers, efforts for economic integration are realistically limited to North-South trade and cooperative investments. Through these efforts, North Korea's industries could become more efficient, and the complementary economies could allocate resources better. The division of labor could increase, and this could enhance gains from trade and eventually close the gap in per capita output.

North-South complementarities are not limited to industrial structure. As is often mentioned, the North possesses high-quality, low-cost labor. Though there are differences in wages according to skill and experience, the average worker receives $40 a month, and a worker for a jointly managed foreign investment firm receives an average of $150 a month (Chun 1993, 105). The level of education of the work force in North Korea is relatively high, and work ethics are well-established. Furthermore, since there are no language barriers, there is more incentive for South Korea to invest here than for other Southeast Asian countries. At a time when South Korea is looking for foreign investment opportunities due to escalating wages at home, investment in the North may just be the right move. The North's proximity would also reduce transportation costs.

Cooperation with the South will teach the North valuable lessons on the workings of the market mechanism. As cooperative investments expand, laws and regulations and financial clearance systems will be required. North Korea's gradual adjustment to these needs will eventually lead down the path of reunification. Most respondents of the survey mentioned above have stated that economic cooperation will speed up

Table 4 Trade between North and South Korea, 1988–94
(thousands of dollars except where noted)

| Year | From North to South | | From South to North | | Total value |
	Number of commodities	Value	Number of commodities	Value	
1988	4	1,037	–	–	1,037
1989	19	22,235	1	69	22,304
1990	26	20,354	4	4,731	25,085
1991	69	165,996	48	26,176	192,172
1992	93	200,685	34	12,818	213,503
1993	87	188,528	39	10,262	198,790
1994		202,000		25,000	227,000

Source: Board of National Unification, 1995, *Monthly Report on North-South Trade & Cooperation* (November).

reunification (Lee 1995). It is a well-known fact that active economic exchanges existed between East and West Germany for more than 20 years before their reunification. As trade and cooperative investments increase and a relationship based on mutual trust develops along with laws and regulations, transfer payments from the South to the North may become possible.

The Present State of North-South Economic Cooperation

South Korea began trading with North Korea in 1989 (table 4). In the first year, South Korea exported $69,000 worth of goods to the North while importing $22.2 million from the North. This imbalance only grew as trading volume increased. The imbalanced trade was a result of North Korea's desire for foreign exchange, not the active exchange of goods. This is further supported by the fact that North Korea imported mostly semiprocessed raw materials for finishing and final export. Trade volume increased rapidly, and by 1991 South Korean exports had risen to $26 million and imports to $166 million. In 1992 the rate of trade growth decreased, with export figures dropping to $12.8 million and imports stopping at $200 million. By this time, however, South Korea had already established itself as an important trading partner of North Korea, accounting for 8 percent of its total trade volume. The nuclear proliferation issue caused a further decrease in trade volume between the two sides by 7 percent in 1993. However, trade volume increased by 14 percent in 1994, showing the possibility for further expansion.

Materials imported into North Korea from the South consist of capital goods such as sock weaving and vacuum packaging machinery; consumer goods such as rice, televisions, and clothes; and semiprocessed

Table 5 Consigned processing trade, 1991–94
(on customs clearance basis)

Year	Cases	Value (thousands of dollars)	Major items
1991	1	23	Student bags
1992	9	529	Bags, rucksacks, clothes, footware
1993	42	4,338	Clothes, furniture, footware
1994[a]	27	12,411	Clothes

a. First nine months.

Source: Board of National Unification, 1995, Monthly Report on North-South Trade & Cooperation (November).

materials such as plasticizers, petrochemicals, and polyester textiles. The current composition of South Korean exports to North Korea shows that once trade with the North becomes liberalized, the opportunity for a more aggressive division of labor will encourage transfer of a considerable amount of capital and semiprocessed material from the South to the North. Furthermore, the lack of consumer goods in North Korea will boost South Korean exports to the North. The South imports mainly agricultural products such as potatoes, traditional medicines, and Alaskan pollock; mineral products such as zinc, gold ingot, pig iron, and hard coal; and consigned processing products such as textiles. The movement of products not only suggests the future division of labor for the two sides but also shows the direction of the flow of materials.

A large percentage of trade between the North and South depends on consigned processing. Consigned processing trade between the two sides began in 1991 and has steadily increased since (table 5). By February 1994, 67 final products, totaling $7.67 million, had been made by means of consigned processing. Calculations from records up to May 1993 show that the value of the reexports is 27 percent higher than that for imported materials.

Since production technology and the quality of labor in North Korea is judged to be satisfactory, consigned processing for light industries is expected to increase. There are, however, certain obstacles. Products need to respond flexibly to changing market conditions, yet the North-South relationship may sour at any time and cause delays in the timely supply of materials.

North Korea has earned a tremendous amount of foreign currency through consigned processing trade with Chochongryun in Japan. In 1992 Japan imported $65 million worth of processed clothes such as men's suits. The superior sewing skills of the North Korean workers and low production costs coupled with technological advice from Chochongryun, which helps maintain the product quality Japanese consumers desire, make North Korea an important clothes supplier to the Japanese market. Since the amendment of the law governing joint ventures in North Korea in 1984, approximately 120 joint ventures with Japanese companies have been launched, most owned by Chochongryun. Germany also imported about $68 million worth of clothes from North Korea in 1992, the bulk of the trade being in consigned processing.

South Korean investments in North Korea have taken the form of consigned processing, with no direct investment so far. South Korean corporate managers who have made several visits to the North voice the possibility of future investments there. Internal political instability in the North, however, has slowed progress. Gradual progress is expected, as North Korea issues its selective invitations. There is no direct trading nor capital investments at this stage due to the less than suitable environment. Once political and military issues are put in order and laws on foreign economic relations are defined, economic exchanges with the South will likely increase. According to a survey by the National Reunification Institute in February 1993, of the 81 South Korean companies that have participated in North-South trading or have met North Koreans for the purpose of promoting economic cooperation, 59 companies (73 percent) have future investments plans in North Korea (*Kyong Hyang Daily*, 11 February 1993).

North Korea has proposed developing a free trade zone in the Najin-Sunbong region as an alternative to China's proposed Tumen River Valley development plan. North Korea is actively preparing for the development of this region, leasing Chungjin harbor to China and making sincere efforts to solidify its position in the shaping of a Northeast Asian economic cooperation framework centered around the Tumen River. In its efforts to gain real economic profits, North Korea has also been looking into developing the Shin-Ui-ju region and Nampo region, which are closer to the heart of China and have better infrastructure. The North has also been working actively to attract foreign investment. However, the lack of infrastructure, laws and regulations, and the current political instability make the environment for investment uncertain. Success in attracting foreign investment has therefore been very limited.

Policies and Issues

Despite the complementarity of the economies and the presence of economic incentives for trade and cooperation, active trade and investment are not taking place. The noneconomic factors impeding mutual exchanges and cooperation are uncertainties and difficulties resulting from differences in political and economic systems. The most important economic factor is the limited North Korean market, which is the main constraint on exports from South to North. Other economic problems are the lack of foreign currency in North Korea, the less-than-established payment clearance system, and the absence of guarantees for investment profit remittance. The lack of infrastructure in North Korea also discourages investment.

However, economic cooperation cannot be furthered through economic problem solving alone. Since economic cooperation involves political factors as well, the two sides need to use economic cooperation as a tool for easing political tension. I have already mentioned that North Korea is very cautious about opening its economy because it is wary of South Korean economic influence and the effects of liberal market forces. At this stage, if the government of the North wishes economic exchanges or cooperation and if the firms of the South are willing, the South Korean government has no reason to disallow it. Such exchanges will benefit both sides but will also help prevent the North from acting irrationally or radically.

Until now, the government of the South has regulated all interactions with the North. The argument was that since the government coordinated all economic activities in the North, the same government control was required in South. This policy, however, often acts to the detriment of both the government and the firm since it prohibits independent decisions and flexible adjustments on the part of the firm and at times may put the government in a rigid position regarding matters that it may prefer to avoid. Therefore, it seems that the government of South Korea should restrict itself to governmental-level economic cooperation and allow firms to make their own decisions. This is not to say that the government should entirely give up its role in cooperation and exchange with the North. The government should seek to establish laws and systems to govern trading and should urge the North Korean government to do the same.

The government should also be careful when it comes to giving incentives to, or sharing the risks of, South Korean firms trading with the North. In addition, the South Korean government should not induce overheated competition in trading with the North by providing discretionary protection and support. Trade based on private judgment should be guaranteed fair access. All exchanges with the North need to be regarded as domestic exchanges, and suitable rules and regulations need to be applied.

Consigned processing is expected to increase at a greater rate than general trading between the two sides. The fact that North Korea has consigned processing contracts not only with the South but also with Japan and Germany implies that the current economic conditions in North Korea are favorable for this type of activity. In other words, the combination of high-quality North Korean labor and developed-country technology and capital promotes economic gains. Consigned processing trade will in the long run prove influential in adjusting the industrial structure of both the North and South. A good example is the labor-intensive textile industry, in which South Korea is interested in competing in the international market. If capital and technology were to be transferred to the North, both the North and South would benefit. Restraining consigned processing trade is undesirable for South Korea. Despite government restraints due to the nuclear dispute in 1994, consigned processing trade with the North has increased, demonstrating that North-South trade can expand even without government protection.

As military tension eases and active reforms take shape in the North, the government of the South should keep the focus on economic integration, investing in infrastructure development, which is of benefit to both the North and the South.

With the conclusion of talks between North Korea and the United States, economic exchanges between the two countries are expected to intensify. Amid preparations by many American firms looking to invest in North Korea, the US government is also preparing to expand trade with North Korea. North Korean assets in the United States, once frozen, have now been freed, and the American government has allowed the export of wheat and rice to North Korea. Better relations between the United States and North Korea will mean better relations between Japan and North Korea. Japanese firms have already made basic preparations for extension into North Korea. Once legal matters are settled, Japanese firms will begin to increase consigned processing trade and to invest in the free trade zone.

The expansion of US and Japanese trade with North Korea will promote economic reform and the opening of North Korean markets. This will naturally increase the likelihood of a North-South reunification scenario.

North Korea's relations with the United States and Japan will contribute to the expansion of economic cooperation between the North and South. Joint extensions of South Korean firms into North Korea with US and Japanese firms will greatly reduce the risks to South Korean firms of North Korea's unpredictable behavior.

These multilateral ventures into North Korea will be beneficial to Japanese and US firms alike. But it will be extremely difficult for American firms to succeed without the help of their South Korean counterparts. South Korean participation solves not only the language barrier problem, it will also enable the use of South Korea's management skills in the North Korean economy. This will help North Korea to use its labor force more effectively. These multilateral efforts are also desirable on North Korea's part because they allow it to overcome feelings of hostility and suspicion toward South Korea. If North Korea were to receive financial support from international institutions such as the World Bank or the Asian Development Bank for projects to be carried out with the United States and South Korea, ideological issues would likely be more easily resolved, ensuring the stability of South Korean investment in the

North. The Tumen River Valley development project is also meaningful for North-South economic cooperation, as it offers a framework for multilateral cooperation.

Once the North Korean government carries out economic reforms and attempts economic development, the government and firms of the South should share management skills, information, and past experiences with the North. Eventually, a single economic system on the Korean peninsula will take root.

Summary and Conclusion

In this chapter, I examined the economic realities of North Korea, analyzed the costs and benefits of economic integration of the North and South, and attempted to define the policy issues for North-South exchanges and economic cooperation as the first step for economic integration.

The economic difficulties of North Korea basically stem from the inefficiencies of socialism and a closed economy, and the breakdown of the old socialist cooperative system centered around the former Soviet Union. The economic problems of North Korea can only be solved by a gradual introduction of the market economy system and the opening of the economy. This, however, will not be an easy task in light of the political instability of North Korea.

The economic conditions in North Korea will eventually render economic reform and opening inevitable and bring about economic integration on the Korean peninsula. Citizens of the South will shoulder a significant portion of the economic burden while the citizens of the North will realize an output 2.5 times the amount of income-opportunity lost by the people of the South. This income gain in North Korea justifies the efforts for economic integration. The increased income should be shared among the citizens of the two sides, but this depends on whether economic cooperation is carried out in a spirit of altruism or whether the South demands partial compensation.

In order to realize economic integration, economic aid from South to North is inevitable. However, the existing Cold War atmosphere between the two sides renders the required support quite unlikely. The most basic cooperative relationship revolves around interaction and cooperation through mutual exchanges and investment. Although efforts for economic cooperation are currently being made, the lack of laws and regulations, a relationship built on mistrust, and discretionary actions of authorities are obstructing the expansion of meaningful cooperation. In order to resolve these issues, authorities of the South should allow exchanges with the North to occur voluntarily at the nongovernmental level and employ a strategy to induce the North Korean government to set up the needed laws and regulations and to expand trade. The expansion of economic cooperation will not only invigorate the North Korean economy but will also prove most effective in bringing about systemic changes in North Korea's economy.

The strategy of expanding the cooperative relationship through multilateral cooperation may prove more effective than unilateral efforts, given that the relationship of trust with North Korea has yet to solidify. American and Japanese firms' extensions into North Korea will promote economic reform and market opening and will most probably further North-South economic cooperation. Furthermore, joint ventures between American and Korean companies will be beneficial for both North and South Korea by increasing the opportunity for North-South economic cooperation. Active South Korean interest in the Tumen River Valley development project, in which North Korea is participating, and cooperation and investment in the Najin-Sunbong region, which it is actively promoting, will help North Korea overcome its international isolation. A strategy focused on making North Korea a participant in the world market will promote economic integration on the Korean peninsula.

References

Bank of Korea. 1994. *Report on Estimation of North Korean GNP*. Seoul.

Board of National Unification. 1994. *Monthly Report on North-South Trade and Cooperation*. (November). Seoul.

Chun, Hong Taek. 1993. "Investment Environment of North Korea and Investment Strategy." In *Investment Environment and Policy Issues in North-South Economic Cooperation*. Seoul: Korean Development Institute.

Economist Intelligence Unit. 1994. *Country Report: South Korea and North Korea*. London.

Hansei Policy Institute. 1994. *North Korean Economy Monthly*. (December).

Kim, You Chan. 1993. "An Economic Evaluation of German Reunification." Korean Institute for Taxation.

Lee, Young-Sun. 1995. "Is Korean Unification Possible?" *Korea Focus on Current Topics* 3, no. 3 (May-June): 3-21.

Lee, Young-Sun. 1994. "Economic Integration of the Korean Peninsula: A Scenario Approach to the Cost of Reunification." In Sung Young Kwack, *The Korean Economy at a Crossroad: Development Prospects, Liberalization, and South-North Economic Integration*. Praeger.

Park, Dong Wun. 1994. "Unification of the Korean Peninsula and Costs of unification." *Studies on Northern Economies* 5: 63-77.

4

Security and Economic Implications of Korean Unification

ROBERT ZOELLICK

My comments cover four areas: the North Korean context; the objectives for the United States and Korea on the one hand, and also for North Korea; a brief assessment of the nuclear agreement; and suggestions on how to work from that agreement.

While there is clearly much we don't know about North Korea, an interesting picture emerges from the information we can glean. Perhaps first and foremost, North Korea remains an extraordinarily militarized economy and society. Even without nuclear weapons, it's a very dangerous nation. And the threat has not diminished over time. It has an army of 1.1 million in a society with a little over 20 million people—the highest ratio of troops to population in the post–Cold War world. Indeed, it rivals the mobilization levels of World War II combatants at their peak. Seventy percent of those forces are deployed within 60 miles of the Demilitarized Zone (DMZ), and North Korean missiles and artillery put the city of Seoul, a quarter of the Republic of Korea's population, and a third of Korean industrial capacity at constant risk. Also at risk are nuclear energy reactors in South Korea—a nuclear issue totally separate from the nuclear weapons problem that gets the most attention. In addition, we presume that the North Koreans have chemical and possibly biological weapons, and we know they have a missile capability that they are trying to enhance.

Robert Zoellick served as undersecretary of state and White House deputy chief of staff in the Bush administration. This chapter represents a transcript of his remarks at the 1995 meeting of the Korea–US Twenty-First Century Council.

This militarization has become a tremendous burden for the North Korean economy and the society. The cost is high not only in terms of resources but also in terms of North Korea's heightening distrust of others. Indicators such as the lack of oil supplies give evidence of reduced military effectiveness, particularly in the air force and armored forces. Nevertheless, the North Korean military remains an extraordinarily powerful threat.

The North Korean economy has been organized to serve the state and the military. Consequently, it is under strain, as the North Korean leadership knows: they stopped reporting annual industrial growth in 1982. Evidence suggests that industrial production has declined in recent years.

More defectors are reporting food shortages, despite supposedly bumper crops in 1993; undoubtedly the shortage of fertilizer is hurting yields. Grain imports have risen considerably since 1990. In the early 1990s, North Korea imported large amounts of wheat from Australia and Canada. Since then, it has shifted more toward corn from China. Given North Korean preferences for wheat as a feed grain, this suggests the country also is experiencing hard-currency shortages.

It appears that consumption of oil is down 25 to 33 percent in 1991–92 versus 1989–90; there are also declines for consumption of coal and coke. The oil scarcity can be traced to the problems in North Korea's trade relationships with Russia—specifically, the subsidies have been phased out, especially those for oil. The change over the last 10 years has been precipitous: a boom in exports from the Soviet Union began after Kim Il Sung's visit to Moscow in 1984, but trade began to fall off in 1988 and plummeted in 1991. This pattern also holds for commodities other than oil. Twenty-five percent of Russian exports to North Korea had been machinery and equipment. China has tried to make up some of this gap but clearly hasn't filled it.

This international economic context has led to further strains on defense, advanced weapons, machinery, and basic transportation. Indeed, the North Korean Communist Party admitted to these problems in its communiqué of December 1993 marking the end of its latest seven-year plan, tracing them to international events. It is not common for Communist Party communiqués to admit any problems at all, much less to refer to the acute situation created by international changes. Further, in 1994 Kim Il Sung acknowledged "grave" challenges to the economy and purged senior economic officials. The Party set the next two to three years as a period of adjustment, giving priority to agriculture, light industries, and trade.

But North Korea clearly does not have an economy with self-correcting features, even for planners. Beginning in the 1970s, the state planning commission was denied statistical information related to the military sector, which, given its share of the economy, is obviously a key omission. Even those of us trained in market economics recognize that planning an economy without facts is indeed a challenge.

North Korean reforms throughout the 1980s strike me as tinkering; they do not represent the initiation of Chinese-style market socialism. Some of the developments in the 1990s, however, may be important for political as well as economic reasons. One such development is the initiation of the free economic and trade zone in the northeast part of North Korea. This zone will require enormous infrastructure investment.

Another development is the possible creation of a dual economy in North Korea. A Russian diplomat who served in North Korea for four years described the emergence of a preferential special sector—a sort of court economy to meet the demands of the new elite. By his estimates, which are unverified, this new court economy might involve about 15 percent of industrial production and 30 to 40 percent of exports. North Korea may be trying, in another form, to build on the model of South Korean conglomerates—perhaps as a vehicle for joint ventures. In this regard, a reference in an April 1993 "Ten-Point Program of Great Unity" is interesting. The tenth point, according to the English translation, reads: These efforts are for "those who have contributed to the great unity of the nation . . . they should be highly estimated." Lest this be deemed too vague, a May 1993 broadcast explained the point further: "What is important in appraising people is, above all, to grant special favors to those who have performed feats for the great unity of the nation and the reunification of the country, political martyrs, and their descendants." This new economic superstructure is a very curious development, and I suspect it could put even greater strains on the basic economy. But it might also become a vehicle for enhanced interaction with the South and others.

Despite North Korea's economic slide, there is no evidence of serious political opposition. Unlike other Marxist-Leninist parties, the Korean Workers Party is truly a mass party, with an estimated 3 million members—that is, one out of seven adults is a member. Observers also cannot ignore the effects of an intense, incessant ideological campaign in an isolated environment. As Young-Sun Lee noted, the North Korean case is very different from that of East Germany, whose citizens nightly watched TV broadcasts from the Federal Republic of Germany; there was far greater exposure to a capitalist democracy in the German case. Nevertheless, losing its founding head of state will undoubtedly create some uncertainty in North Korea, a topic to which I will return later in discussing the political environment.

Internationally, the decline in North Korea's trade relations was part of a larger slide toward greater isolation. Here, the Republic of Korea deserves extraordinary credit for a very able *Nordpolitik*, which led to its recognition by the Soviet Union in 1990, the People's Republic of China in 1992, and the dual admission to the United Nations in 1991, which

North Korea has long opposed. Those developments, combined with the fall of communist regimes, clearly had an effect on North Korea's view of its international position. Indeed, its economic and international problems may have led the North Koreans to explore what it could gain from nuclear weapons development and the subsequent negotiations to eliminate them. It is no accident that North Korea accepted the December 1991 agreements between the North and South on political reconciliation and denuclearization of the peninsula but then stalled the implementing protocols. Similarly, in 1992, six years after signing the nuclear Non-Proliferation Treaty, North Korea finally agreed to International Atomic Energy Agency inspections, but then resisted further inquiries after the investigations revealed discrepancies.

In sum, North Korea faces an economic decline, international isolation, and political transition. In addition, it has demonstrated a willingness to use violence, especially to destabilize the South.

Yet while this country's behavior strikes the world as outside the range of what is normal and acceptable, it ought not be classified as out of control or suicidal. The regime's efforts to destabilize its opponents send a signal: "Don't tread on me." Further, if we can draw anything from past experience, the pattern of communist regimes is to seek a period of relaxed tensions after a leadership change. The North Koreans know they have economic problems, but they are in a bind because they fear the opening of North Korean society to foreign influence. It is not clear if they are buying time for the succession, slipping into an accelerating decline, or trying to develop some alternative strategy of international interaction.

Objectives in US-Korean Relations

It is hard to talk about a nation's policies unless you have a sense of its objectives. Security of the Republic of Korea, now and in the future, seems the obvious first goal. The 37,000 US troops are of course key to realizing it, but security also means preparing for contingencies, be it aggression, crisis, or the collapse of North Korea.

The second objective is to enhance the credibility of the US defense commitment to Japan, which is the keystone of regional stability and the US role in Asia. It is worth emphasizing that the US commitment to Korea is part of an overall strategy for the security of East Asia. Former Singapore Prime Minister Lee Kuan Yew hit the nail on the head when he said there is no natural balance of power in East Asia. The United States creates that stability in the region. As Koreans know well, China, Japan, and Russia's past spheres of influence have all concentrated on incorporating the peninsula. Consequently, the overall US-Korean security relationship has to fit within this larger commitment to sustaining a regional balance of power.

A third objective is maintaining the integrity of global nonproliferation regimes. This is not only a matter of dealing with North Korea, but also of preventing the export of dangerous nuclear materials.

A fourth objective is peaceful normalization, reconciliation, and democratization, which involves the democratic reunification of Korea.

What is striking about these four objectives is that they are neither solely peninsular nor solely international. They are intermeshed and inseparable. Thus, we must take them into account simultaneously as we proceed.

What are the North Koreans' objectives? First, North Korea is seeking stronger political legitimacy, and that especially means recognition by the United States. Second, it wants to enhance its security. This in part could be achieved through assurance against attack but probably also, in a very practical sense, through reduced Korean-US forces.

North Korea must be seeking economic benefits as well, but this objective is complicated by the dangers it perceives in increased openness. Such openness would threaten its legitimacy as a state because it would clearly undercut 50 years of propaganda about an impoverished South. It would also increase North Korea's illegitimacy in another way: if North Korea turned to capitalist practices, its citizens would start to wonder about its reason for being.

On this question of legitimacy, there is an interesting analogy to be drawn from the German experience. During 1989–90, the East Germans saw West Germany as the legitimate state. When unification was imminent, it took place, significantly, under a clause of the West German constitution that allowed for annexation or absorption. Another clause, backed by some East German intellectuals, would have allowed a merger creating a new constitutional arrangement, but the East German people wanted nothing of it. They viewed West Germany as the legitimate state, and that legitimacy was based on its economic success and political freedom. Also, these East German intellectuals and other analysts apparently underestimated the importance of the fact that their nation had been created by a foreign power, the Soviet Union.

In 1989, after the Berlin Wall fell, I visited some Lutheran ministers who had courageously led early East German reform efforts. They wanted to create a third way, neither capitalist nor communist, and were saddened when they had to admit that the average East German wanted nothing more than that which his West German brothers and sisters had.

It is unclear the degree to which North Koreans have a similar understanding of South Korean society, but certainly they have much less than was the case among Germans. Thus, economic interaction represents both an opportunity for the North Korean regime and also a potential risk.

I also would expect that North Korea will seek to further its political, security, and economic objectives by sowing distrust among the Republic of Korea, the United States, and others. Thus, it will likely seek to retain ambiguity about its nuclear capability, whether as insurance or blackmail.

Implications of the Nuclear Pact

How does the recent nuclear agreement affect this situation? While it is not my purpose to argue for or against it, I will try to touch on its effects, and in a manner that is as neutral as possible.

First, the agreement will take a long time to execute. During that time, the United States and others will directly engage North Korea. In particular, it will take at least five years to determine North Korea's nuclear capability. It will take another eight years or more to dismantle current capabilities. Before then, whatever capability North Korea has will remain intact. In addition, we can't stop what we can't find.

Another element of the agreement is the interconnectedness of its provisions and its conditional obligations, principally involving the North, the South, and the United States. Even nonexpert readers of the agreement can see that there are possibilities for ambiguity. The North Korean pattern is obvious: they will be obstinate, they will resist, and they will try to marginalize the South in the process. Technical issues will continue to become political disputes. In addition, the agreement will open North Korea to outside influences and possible economic help. Most probably, the economic engagement will involve the Republic of Korea, the United States, and Japan. These three countries must work closely together so as to maintain economic leverage on the North and not to let the North play one off against the others.

It is also significant that the agreement is not linked to dangers related to the conventional posture of the North Korean military. The absence of this connection is unfortunate. But we should not compound the problem by overlooking the conventional dimension as we deal with the nuclear danger in the future.

In short, this agreement is an organized beginning—definitely not an end. Ambassador Robert L. Gallucci has made this point, with the appropriate cautions: compliance with this agreement, or perhaps even extension into other areas such as conventional force posture, will fundamentally depend on North Korea's assessment of its security, political, and economic interests. We shouldn't fool ourselves; if the North perceives the agreement and compliance to be in its interest, it will eventually, grudgingly take steps. If it doesn't, it won't.

Posing a Choice

Finally, what common approaches could the United States and Korea take as regards North Korea? Conceptually, there are two possible strategies. One is to keep North Korea isolated, deter any aggressive acts, and wait for its collapse. Such an approach would appeal to those who oppose "throwing a lifeline" to North Korea. It would also limit North Korea's ability to manipulate others and would avoid legitimating it. However, this approach has some substantial risks: we don't know what North Korea might do in desperation if collapse of its regime was imminent.

The second strategy is to offer engagement, but only if North Korea takes concrete, positive steps. Such a strategy links promotion of a "soft landing" economically to political engagement. It even offers the opportunity to introduce "poison carrots" to North Korean society: that is, a greater degree of economic and social association with the South and the rest of the outside world could weaken the legitimacy of the North Korean regime.

Because the United States and Korea have already chosen this second strategy, the discussion of an alternate strategy may be largely theoretical. But I would offer one additional thought about the two paths: it is important that North Korea view our course as a choice—not the only option open to us. One track offers a set of carefully structured incentives to eventually defuse tensions, build confidence, and promote gradual engagement with the world in economic and political terms. The other track is one of increased isolation and relentless international pressure. If North Korea doesn't play by the rules, we have this alternative of isolation. The US public, as well as the South Korean public, and other international players, China and Japan in particular, need to understand that we have offered North Korea an alternative. By clarifying the understanding of all parties that we retain the alternative of isolation, we will enhance our leverage.

Let me make seven specific suggestions.

The first is a corollary of the strategy. We have to expect and prepare to manage the strategy over many years. Challenges will occur. But it is important to be consistent and constant, and to recognize that we are determining the rules of the engagement with North Korea as we proceed. We are conditioning expectations. How we respond to North Korean actions will determine how the North views its room for maneuver in subsequent situations. This suggestion will require extraordinarily close Korean and US cooperation. Different views are natural, but we should try to work them out in a way that avoids giving North Koreans leverage.

It is also important to recognize that North Korea will use a Stalinist negotiating style: rigid and frustrating, but generally predictable. It is on again and off again. It is inflexible but not necessarily immovable, and that is an important distinction. In my view this style reflects weakness and vulnerability rather than strength.

Second, we must build engagement from a base of deterrence—that is, military preparedness and vigilance with no shortcuts. The North Koreans must recognize that a military buildup, whether conventional or nuclear, is a losing course for them. They know it is a losing proposition in economic terms, but it is the one strength they think they have. We need to make it abundantly clear that a military threat gets the North Koreans nothing.

Third, we should seek to broaden the North Korean nuclear agreement to include contacts with the Republic of Korea and the United States on conventional military issues. I agree with Hakjoon Kim: we want to reduce tensions with phased confidence-building measures. Such measures could deal with topics such as mutual reduction and eventual elimination of armaments within the DMZ and mutual force reductions of heavy armaments within a certain distance of the DMZ.

Given Seoul's geographic position, any changes of this sort would have to be asymmetrical. We should be striving for equal security, not necessarily identical measures. The efforts could include aspects that have been used in the European context, such as transparency, advance notification of exercises, and observers.

South Korea should not view the nuclear agreement as putting it at a disadvantage in any way. After all, the South has many assets. It should be taking the offensive in terms of diplomacy and in terms of prodding the North Koreans. Such an offensive would not be intended to score points internationally, but would show the North Koreans that South Korea is extending an alternative path that is open if the North wants it, even while Korean security is preserved.

Fourth, Korea needs to cultivate a supportive external environment— in effect, to build diplomatic and economic assets in preparation for what might come. Such support would be needed under crisis conditions, or for leverage, or to isolate the North Koreans. Korea built such support ably through opening relations with the Soviet Union and China. The United States helped Korea achieve these openings by providing contacts with Gorbachev's government and also through the Asia Pacific Economic Cooperation (APEC) forum, which became a device for bringing together China, Taiwan, and Hong Kong. In particular, Korea should focus on enhancing its relationships with the United States, China, Japan, and Russia.

In the case of the United States, I cannot emphasize enough the importance of building trust. Trust comes over time, not only from joint handling of major issues, but from continuous sharing of information. This trust must be built not only with officials, but also with the US public. If there are crises sparked by North Korea getting off the track we have designed, as is likely at some point, the United States will need to act as a diplomatic catalyst, just as it did in the case of German unification, and there must be broad support of this role.

The need for public support poses a challenge for both Korea and the

US government. With the end of the Cold War, Korea ought not to take US public attitudes for granted. The United States will look at a whole series of issues in evaluating its relationship with Korea. The US public is not isolationist. The Times Mirror surveys of both US opinion leaders and the general public have shown that, if led properly, Americans appreciate the importance of international relationships. But Americans also develop their own sense of Korean objectives and policies from reading newspapers and watching the television news; Korean officials ought to keep that in mind.

The relationship with China is obviously also critical. China has become a lifeline for North Korea. Despite this, South Korea has very ably extended its relations with China. But we must recognize that China's political transition will not be an easy period for any of us.

Korea's relationship with Japan, obviously, is a highly sensitive topic. But it is one on which the United States and Korea must carefully cooperate. When in 1991 a leader of Japan's LDP proposed a relationship with North Korea outside the foreign ministry channel, US and Korean pressure helped push that effort back into line. But as the Republic of Korea starts to explore enhanced economic ties with the North, the Japanese will want to do so as well. I suggest that Koreans should work with the United States to avoid a situation in which Japan develops an economic relationship with North Korea and South Korea does not, due to resistance from the North. We want to avoid a situation in which Japan has a special link to North Korea and the United States has a special link to South Korea. While this scenario is not probable, it underscores the importance of Korean consultations with the United States and Japan. Japan, too, is in a period of political transition, so it is crucial that Korea and the United States handle this carefully and delicately together.

I would draw another analogy from the German unification process: it was absolutely critical for Germany that events unfolded within secure trans-Atlantic and European frameworks. One of our basic strategic themes was to unify Germany within the framework of Western structures and institutions: the European Union and NATO. Similarly, it will be important for Korea that there are structures in place to assure other nations that unification is not a threat to their security. This may seem somewhat odd advice for Korea, given its history of vulnerability to security threats from China, Russia, and Japan. But it would be foolish to think that any major change in Korean security or political relationships would not create tremors in the region. The best way to manage those tremors is to have structures in place in advance.

The fifth point relates to the need for an institutional structure on the economic side. Economic relationships can help develop a sense of common interest and a base of support. Organizations such as the APEC forum and the World Trade Organization (WTO) are very important for Korea in terms of demonstrating mutuality of interests with others and promoting trust through increased interaction. At some point Korea will need the help of other countries, or at least their acceptance of a process to deal with North Korea. When that happens, having built up some "capital" with these countries will be important.

One appropriate starting point could be international contacts through the World Bank, International Monetary Fund, or Asian Development Bank on issues relating to reunification. Of course, South Korea will want to have strong influence if these organizations become involved in North Korea. Such contacts may offer an opportunity for increased South Korean interaction with the North, but perhaps in a framework that makes it easier for North Korea to move toward a policy of reconciliation.

Sixth, South Korea must enhance the flexibility of its domestic economy. The German case has created much apprehension in Korea, but Korea can profit from the German experience. Specifically, Germany faced several difficulties that South Korea could avoid. One is that the wage rates in East Germany were too high given the productivity levels. Second, the German decision on how to handle property rights created investment uncertainty. A third element, which Korea will also have to determine how to resolve, is the degree of rigidity in the social welfare system. Over the course of 45 to 50 years, Germany developed many such rigidities. Applying these to East Germany threatened to sap the economic vitality West Germany enjoyed during its takeoff decades earlier.

Beyond heeding these warnings of potential pitfalls, Korea should also recognize the real opportunities in terms of reduced military spending, modernization of industry, labor availability, and, if it creates conditions friendly to foreign direct investment, good rates of return.

Both the benefits and costs of reunification will revolve around whether the Republic of Korea deals with its structural economic distortions: that is, whether it maintains protection in the agriculture sector or modernizes it and reallocates the labor force to more productive sectors; whether Korea continues the artificial segmentation of the capital market and preferential access to and allocation of capital; whether it supports business conglomerates to the detriment of its underdeveloped small-business and service industry sectors; whether it ends extralegal government intervention in business decisions in favor of the application of the impartial, predictable rule of law; and whether Korea develops a positive environment for foreign direct investment. These issues affect not only Korea's economic vitality as it faces reunification but also the level of its political support from other nations.

Seventh and perhaps most important, the United States and the Republic of Korea must be steadfast in creating a dialogue between South and North. North Korea must accept not only South Korea's right to exist, but eventually its legitimacy as well. We know they will resist. We know from everything in their history and from recent events that they will seek to circumvent South Korea. We should not accept any deal that permits it. In the end, the path of engagement may not produce reconciliation and may not defuse the danger. Thus, the Republic of Korea and the United States must be ready to manage the situation; they must be ready for a crisis. Maximum diplomatic and economic assets must be summoned to this task, though they will have to be developed over time. International support is key in this endeavor, and the trust and support of the US government and its public will prove invaluable as well.

II

KOREA–US ECONOMIC RELATIONSHIP

5

US–Korea Economic Relations

DANIEL K. TARULLO

At present, the most important determinant of US-Korean economic relations is how Korea will resolve its ambivalence toward economic liberalization and more complete integration into the world economy. If Korea resolves this ambivalence in favor of greater openness and participation in international institutions, the US-Korean economic relationship is likely to prosper, US investment in Korea will increase, and trade problems will be easier to rectify.

If, on the other hand, Korea decelerates its pace of liberalization and retains more insular economic policies, the bilateral economic relationship is likely to be both less significant and more problematic. US investment will flow much more readily to other parts of Asia, and trade disputes will linger and perhaps even multiply.

In this chapter, I will explain the US perception of Korean ambivalence toward liberalization as a prelude to discussing the present and future of the bilateral economic relationship.

Korea: Challenge and Choices

As is well known, Korea's rapid economic growth began in the early 1960s, when the government abandoned its ineffective policy of import substitution in favor of an export-led strategy. It devalued the won and implemented a variety of policies to nurture exporters: cash subsidies,

---

Daniel K. Tarullo is assistant secretary of state for economic and business affairs.

permission to retain foreign exchange earnings, exemptions from virtually all import controls, and favorable access to credit.

In the 1970s the Korean government launched a drive to develop heavy industries such as steel, machinery, shipbuilding, and chemicals through an explicit industrial policy whose elements included favorable credit allocation, tax incentives, import protection, and tolerance of high industry concentration ratios; *chaebols* prospered under these policies.

The performance of the Korean economy since basic import substitution policies were dropped has clearly been spectacular. In the last 30 years, annual growth has averaged nearly 9 percent. Korea is one of the top 15 exporters in the world, with an economy more than two-thirds as large as those of OECD member states.

These highly interventionist and frequently protectionist industrial policies are usually thought to have spawned this period of rapid growth. Whatever their relative contribution to Korea's past economic success, the remnants of these policies now limit the expansion and competitiveness of the Korean economy. Industrial policy further strengthened the already-powerful Korean bureaucracy, burdening the economy with layers of formal and informal controls. The financial system was thin and inefficient, having been used principally to allocate credit to favored undertakings or sectors. A related problem was the emergence of high inflation levels, as credit was continuously channeled to government-supported basic industries.

In the 1980s Korea undertook a variety of economic reforms, such as tariff reductions, bank privatization, and a measure of financial liberalization. Strong anti-inflationary measures were also taken. Significant as these changes were, they only were the beginning of this task of genuine economic liberalization. When rapid growth resumed later in the decade, pressure for reform dissipated.

The year 1992 saw a significant economic downturn. As President Kim Young Sam took office in 1993, many influential Koreans believed that the structural limits of highly interventionist economic policies had been reached. Korea had lost its low-cost labor advantage as wages had risen. Productivity gains slowed as Korean firms failed to make efficiency gains in an overregulated economy in which oligopolistic firms remained dominant. Despite significant investment in technology, there were therefore serious questions as to whether many Korean companies could be world-class competitors.

In these circumstances, President Kim initiated his program of economic reform, including controversial measures such as real-name disclosure in the financial sector. The Kim plan called for reduced government control throughout the economy. It also called for further internationalization of the Korean economy. Shortly thereafter, Presidents Kim and Clinton agreed to the Dialogue for Economic Cooperation, which I will discuss below.

There have certainly been some reforms in the last two years, and President Kim has recently reiterated his call for globalization. But many suspect that the economic reform movement has slowed and perhaps even stalled. Breaking with traditions of bureaucratic guidance is not easy. And while globalization may seem an imperative in some respects, it cuts against the grain of an economy in which foreigners sometimes seem quite unwelcome.

It appears to us that there is a measure of "reform fatigue" in Seoul, grounded in the view that the moderate reforms to date may be sufficient to adjust Korea's economy and that further breaks with past policies and traditions are unnecessary. Here is where we detect ambivalence: globalization and the necessary accompanying liberalization are an attractive route to growth and a threat to policies and practices that appear to have served Korea well.

This ambivalence is captured in some contrasting statistics. On the one hand, Korea's growth rate has rebounded to around 8 percent, an admirable figure by nearly any standard. On the other hand, the Institute for International Management Development's assessment of world competitiveness ranks Korea 24th out of 41 countries surveyed. Perhaps more disturbing, Korea's competitiveness among the 18 developing countries surveyed has fallen from third in 1991 to seventh in 1994.

The Dialogue for Economic Cooperation

At the outset of the Kim Young Sam and Clinton administrations in 1993, Korea was known as one of the toughest places for foreigners to do business. Through "policy loans" and restrictions on foreign exchange, the government still directed or tightly controlled capital flows. The financial system was underdeveloped, the foreign investment approval process was unpredictable, and foreign companies could not own land. The legacy of over 30 years of Korean government promotion of manufacturing and exports and its "frugality campaigns" lingered in the public mind and in many government regulations and practices.

Until very recently, Korea's push for globalization and economic openness was geared almost exclusively toward export-led growth. This approach is no longer sufficient to sustain rapid economic development. Korea's economy is at a structural crossroads; production of basic manufactured goods, such as shoes and textiles, are moving to other, lower-cost Asian markets. This is a sign of Korea's progress and of its opportunity to evolve from a newly industrialized economy to a more advanced economy, where workers' skills are rewarded with a higher standard of living and access to the world's best products.

Greater investment from all sources will be needed to maintain Korea's growth and economic transformation. Yet as President Kim took office, Korea still appeared not to welcome foreign direct investment. Although foreign investment helps disseminate capital, technology, and know-how, significant institutional barriers remain. Burdensome, nontransparent regulations and local requirements added time and cost to investment transactions. In fact, foreign direct investment has long accounted for a smaller proportion of total national investment than in any other high growth Asian economy.

The Clinton administration strongly supported the intentions of President Kim and other senior officials to liberalize Korea's economy. The reasons are twofold: first, the United States wants Korea, an important strategic ally, to continue as a strong and vibrant participant in the global economy. Second, a more open Korean economy will forsake many of the government practices that thwart US businesses in Korea and produce bilateral trade irritants.

In order to support the Kim government's liberalization effort and to ensure that the views of US business were included in this effort, the Clinton administration entered into a new dialogue with Korea last year. This dialogue was, in essence, a test of whether a less confrontational approach could accelerate and deepen domestic forces for liberalization. The administration chose Korea as a test case because President Kim demonstrated a high-level commitment to globalization and economic liberalization. US officials were heartened by President Kim's promise to make Korea "the best place in the world to do business." The US-Korea Economic Subcabinet agreed to launch an intensive two-way dialogue on economic issues in June 1993. This effort, known as the Dialogue for Economic Cooperation (DEC), was endorsed by Presidents Clinton and Kim the following month.

I do not want to overemphasize the importance of the DEC experiment. It was not meant to replace multilateral, regional, or bilateral trade policy efforts. Rather, the one-year dialogue was intended to be a temporary supplement to the more traditional market-access talks. But neither do I want to minimize the significance of the attempt to encourage and assist domestic forces of economic liberalization through DEC.

Although the US business community was interested in this dialogue, Korea's stakes were even greater. The government of Korea had become concerned that Korea was losing new investments to other Pacific Rim countries with more hospitable conditions. Moreover, some established major foreign investors withdrew from Korea to seek better opportunities elsewhere. The Korean government saw in the DEC an opportunity to engage in a dialogue about economic reform as a means of accelerating implementation of its globalization policies.

Although the dialogue was quite broad, the talks focused on reducing impediments to foreign investment flows and improving the climate for foreign investors after establishment. US officials resisted the effort to concentrate on quick fixes and attempted to devote time and effort to more systemic problems.

Implementation of the DEC is not complete. Thus, my assessment is necessarily a provisional one. Still, let me highlight a few areas covered in the DEC.

Visible impediments to investment have been only modestly reduced to date. The investment screening process was streamlined, but the Korean government was unwilling to eliminate it completely. In the past, many bureaucrats have used this application process to delay or thwart foreign investors. Faced with daunting bureaucratic hurdles, many foreign companies have decided to go to other, more attractive markets in Asia.

A few sectors formerly closed to foreign investors were opened, but many industrial sectors of interest to US firms remain effectively off-limits. For example, although Korea now allows foreigners to invest in foreign language schools, investment is limited to 49 percent of equity in one model school per market. Although the Korean government agreed to allow foreign firms to provide various ground handling services in Korea, most of these service sectors are also subject to 49 percent foreign equity limitations and to certain regulatory exceptions.

Another example is cargo loading and unloading services, which are limited to firms with no more than 49 percent foreign equity. The 1 January 1995 liberalization of freight agency and brokerage services excludes air freight. And according to what the local airport authority recently told an American firm, approval for activities under the 1 July 1994 opening of the operation of air terminal facilities sector is applicable only to investments in the new Seoul airport, which is not scheduled for completion until 2002.

Turning to practices affecting investment postestablishment, the Korean government passed a basic law for administrative regulations that provides for transparency in implementation of administrative law and the opportunity for public comment on new rules. The government also established an ombudsman-like council to hear citizen complaints against arbitrary government actions. I understand that in several hundred cases the council has ruled against the government. Although it will take time to change the attitudes of the government bureaucrats, the Ministry of Government Affairs is actively training government officials regarding their new obligations to the public.

Under DEC auspices, the Department of Justice and the Korean Fair Trade Commission initiated an active dialogue regarding government policies to ensure fair competition. Korea agreed to relax restrictions on sales promotion, thereby allowing market newcomers (including foreign firms) to use innovative sales promotion tools. It also improved access to television advertising by new entrants into the market. The United States agreed to train Korean investigators in investigation of unfair trade practice complaints in order to ensure that Korean firms do not abuse their market power.

US and Korean tax authorities negotiated a memorandum of understanding on how to resolve tax disputes and on taxation of overseas subsidiaries. This agreement resolves some of the uncertainty faced by Korean and US firms investing in each other's markets.

In addition to these longer-term efforts, Korea agreed to specific steps to help establish investors in Korea. For example, the government eased restrictions on holding of land and access to domestic financing.

Again, I do not want to overstate what the DEC accomplished. The dialogues on administrative procedures and competition policy have not caused a sea change in Korean bureaucratic or business attitudes toward foreign competitors. They have, however, provided the Korean government with new tools for accelerating its globalization drive. Certainly, with President Kim Young Sam's determination to push internationalization, administrative deregulation in Korea has taken on a new vigor. Foreign investors have already seen some improvement in Korea's investment climate. More is needed. If the new government uses these tools aggressively, foreign investors will detect an improvement in Korea's business climate.

Certainly, the DEC was not an unqualified success. This assessment—that it has been only "modestly successful"—stems partly from the United States' high initial expectations arising from the Kim administration's ringing call for economic reform. The talks were more like a negotiation and less like a cooperative dialogue than US officials, and I suspect the Korean government, would have liked.

The changes implemented by the Korean government represent part of a gradual economic evolution, not the economic policy revolution that President Kim espoused soon after his election. Korea is still far from "the best place in the world to do business." Indeed, the competitiveness report to which I alluded earlier ranked Korea 39th out of 41 countries for its financial sector, 38th for cost of capital, and dead last for local capital markets and cultural openness.

In light of Korea's interest in attracting more international investment, one must ask why this joint effort was not more successful. I think there are two reasons.

First, economic liberalization is politically difficult in any country. Established forces do not want more competition, even if it improves the efficiency of the economy as a whole. Moreover, Korea's DEC efforts were complicated by the distraction of the final year of Uruguay Round negotiations. Korean officials who supported President Kim's economic policy vision were fully occupied with building a domestic consensus in favor of the Uruguay Round agreements—in particular the provisions of the agricultural deal. While Korea's agreement to the Uruguay Round provisions is an important milestone, it may have prevented the Korean government from fully capitalizing on the opportunity that the intensive DEC process represented.

The second reason for less-than-expected progress in the DEC—and this is something of a paradox—was the recovery of Korea's economy. Soon after President Kim came to office, there was a great deal of momentum in favor of economic reform because Korea's economy was mired in a slump. As the economy picked up steam in 1994, however, domestic opponents to liberalization gained strength. Korea's cyclical recovery gave them ammunition to argue that more drastic economic reforms were not needed.

From the standpoint of the United States, the DEC experiment, even with these modest gains, was worthwhile. Although the DEC final report does not match the economic reform rhetoric of the Kim administration, it does improve the business environment for US firms in Korea over the longer term. More importantly, the United States gained experience in conducting talks about economic liberalization with a reform-minded government.

From Korea's standpoint as well, the DEC should not be judged more than modestly successful because the tentative steps to open Korea's economy have not excited foreign investors. While investment from some sources has risen somewhat, there has been no upsurge of investment plans by US business. The US embassy reports that business problems are still widespread. Meanwhile, other countries in East and South Asia are liberalizing at a more rapid pace. In a relative sense, Korea has fallen further behind the competition, and thus American business is more likely to look elsewhere in Asia for investment sites.

The investment climate in Korea should be of much more concern to the Korean government than it is to the United States. US investors have many other investment options, and a hostile investment atmosphere in Korea will only drive them elsewhere.

Bilateral Trade and Investment Problems

There continue to be significant trade problems with Korea. Here again, I believe that a sustained economic liberalization effort will improve matters considerably. Particularly in the case of market-access problems, US officials will continue to insist that US firms be given the same opportunities in Korea that Korean firms enjoy in US markets.

The US Treasury Department and the Korean Ministry of Finance and Economy have discussed financial sector liberalization for many years. These discussions have produced some results. In 1993, for example, Korea broke new ground with its comprehensive *Blueprint for Financial Sector Liberalization*. Implementation of this blueprint has already reached the final stage, as Korea accelerated implementation of a number of measures. Further, late last year the Ministry of Finance and Economy announced its Foreign Exchange System Reform Plan. Korean officials recently met with Treasury representatives in Geneva for financial services negotiations under the World Trade Organization.

Despite all the activity and good intentions, Korea is fast falling behind its Asian neighbors in financial sector liberalization. Foreign banks and securities firms operating in Korea face exceptionally high operating costs and day-to-day problems that limit their range of new products. These problems are quickly fading or have been eliminated in other Asian markets. Indeed, some financial firms claimed that Korea has replaced Japan as the most difficult place for foreign financial institutions to do business. This opinion has only been strengthened since the United States concluded a financial review agreement with Japan in January 1995.

This situation is regrettable for two reasons. First, continued reluctance to open financial markets and modernize the financial sector will inevitably hurt Korea's competitiveness. The day-to-day business problems mentioned earlier are just examples of why Korea risks losing its attractiveness as an investment locale compared with other Asian economies. Development of a modern, sophisticated financial sector is crucial to maintaining a competitive international economy.

Second, the lack of substantive progress in US-Korean financial liberalization talks is regrettable because it seems to lie in stark contrast to the intentions of senior officials at the Blue House. Clearly, the Kim administration has committed itself to the process of economic reform, including liberalization of the financial sector. Korea's goal of attaining OECD membership by 1996, for example, indicates the direction that the Blue House wants to take and the greater role in the global economy it has in mind for Korea. Up to this point, however, this momentum is not being transferred effectively through the bureaucracy. US officials hope, however, that the recent bureaucratic reorganization and the merger of the Economic Planning Board with the Ministry of Finance will help to rectify this problem.

In the trade area, the United States continues to be frustrated with the difficult and grudging nature of the negotiations. While it would be fair to say that visible trade barriers such as tariffs and quotas have steadily diminished over the past decade—a process to be continued by the Uruguay Round agreements, more subtle barriers involving standards, licensing, certification, rule making, and import processing have increased.

Last November, the Office of the US Trade Representative (USTR) accepted a petition filed by the American meat industry that asserts that Korea restricts US meat imports and abrogates several bilateral trade agreements. Of particular concern is the Korean Ministry of Health's mandated shelf-life standards for various types of frozen, chilled, and vacuum-packed meats. Despite repeated attempts to resolve the issue, more than a year went by with no resolution.

Korea's costly and time-consuming regulations on testing of medical devices do not recognize international standards and impose testing requirements that differ by designated laboratory. Moreover, the Korean customs service's insistence on physically inspecting each medical device risks contamination. USTR estimates that these practices disrupt as much as $200 million of US medical equipment exports.

Automobile market access remains a matter of great concern. While talks last year produced some modest progress, little has been done to counteract the legacy of anti-import bias, which until recently included the likelihood that a Korean consumer who purchased a foreign car would be subject to a tax audit.

Whither Korean Economic Liberalization

If one were to look at the individual components of the bilateral economic dialogue—the frustrating financial discussions and endless debates over nontariff barriers—it would be easy to be pessimistic about the US-Korea bilateral economic relationship. On the other hand, if one were to hear only the Korean government's calls for globalization and deregulation, it would be difficult to understand why the bilateral trade and investment talks are so contentious. The future US-Korean economic relationship depends to a great extent upon the Korean government's ability to sustain and implement its liberalization policies.

I was encouraged by President Kim's 1995 New Year's address, in which he stated that "globalization is the shortcut that will lead us to building a first-class country in the 21st century." In addition, the new economic team that President Kim has assembled appears to be quite capable and supportive of economic liberalization.

In light of my experience over the past year, however, I am uncertain whether President Kim's commitment to globalization will be reflected in the thousands of lower-level bureaucratic decisions that affect foreign businesses in Korea. Another problem is what appears to us to be a lack of support for internationalization among the Korean public. It is not clear that Koreans see President Kim's globalization concept as something more than a means for increasing Korea's exports.

For Korea's part, the choice is simple. It can move forward resolutely with a globalization program that will deepen and broaden economic linkages with its trade and investment partners. Alternatively, it could choose to slow the pace of economic liberalization. As foreign investors are free to choose the most promising markets in which to invest, this course of action would leave Korea less attractive than other East Asian economies, which are dramatically reducing barrier to capital flows. Foreign investors are already sending clear signals.

For now, the US perception of ambivalence remains. One recent manifestation of this ambivalence is that Korea has not yet formally submitted its application to the OECD, despite its oft-repeated desire to join by 1996. There are conflicting reports of the reasons for delay. If Korea moves forward, enters the OECD, and conforms to the liberal trade and financial regimes that are requisite for admission, American and other foreign investors will take notice. US officials were encouraged by Korea's small move to raise the ceiling on foreign ownership of shares in quoted companies from 10 to 12 percent. But if Korea holds back, implements only modest reforms, or treats the admission process as a contentious negotiation, Korea's image in the international business community will not improve.

There is an old custom in Korea to paste auspicious Chinese-character couplets on one's door on *ipchoon*, the first day of spring. As Koreans celebrated this holiday in 1995, many of them pasted signs on their doors that stated, "Open the door, open for ten thousand blessings; sweep the earth, sweep for gold." I am told that the reverse of this traditional saying has been summed up in the Korean proverb "to close the door to a blessing," which is used to refer to someone who closes his door to a business opportunity. At this point in the maturing US-Korean bilateral relationship, Korea has the opportunity to open new doors. If it does not, we may never know the blessings that will be missed.

6

KOREA–US ECONOMIC RELATIONS IN THE 1990s: CONFLICT OR COOPERATION?

SOOGIL YOUNG

The first meeting of the Korea–United States Twenty-First Century Council meeting, held in February 1994, considered the bilateral economic relations between the two countries and exposed a wide perception gap between the two countries concerning the health of those relations. The meeting was adjourned without resolving the issue. This chapter further explores and attempts to resolve this problem.

In 1994 the Korean participants came to the meeting with the view that, although ridden with many small problems, Korean-US economic relations were basically sound. Accordingly, they were more or less surprised to hear some of their American counterparts voice the view that, during recent years, Korea had failed to show any real progress in opening up its economy to foreign imports and investment. Given the Americans' view, the two countries were bound to collide sooner or later (Krause 1994). Needless to say, the accuracy of this view has to be ascertained, even if rather belatedly.

The importance of Korean-US economic relations has declined during the last several years. The US share of Korea's total trade peaked at 30 percent in 1987 and then declined to 21 percent in 1993. Still, the United States continues to be Korea's largest trading partner. The United States also ranks with Japan as Korea's most important source of advanced technologies and foreign direct investment.

Soogil Young is currently the president of the Korea Transport Institute in Seoul.

With Korea's continued high economic growth, Korean-US economic relations have been steadily gaining in importance for the United States. With its share in US international trade at 3.0 percent in 1993, Korea is the United States' seventh largest trading partner; on the export side alone it places sixth, outranking China, France, and Italy. With its rapidly growing domestic market, Korea's importance as an export market for the United States will continue to grow.

In other words, both countries have a stake in maintaining healthy economic relations. Furthermore, since Korea is the third largest economy as well as the third largest trader in East Asia, Korean-US relations are a very important component in trans-Pacific economic relations, with a significant bearing on their evolution. From these perspectives, it will be important to further cooperative relations and avoid conflictual ones between Korea and the United States. The relevant question for the two countries and for this chapter, of course, is how to achieve this balance.

The Evolution of Korean-US Economic Relations

Modern Korean-US relations date back to the late 1940s, when after liberation from Japanese occupation, Korea became a protégé of the United States and a defense against communist aggression. For the next 30 years or so, security issues dominated Korean-US relations. Economic relations evolved essentially as a means to support the security relationship and took the form of US development assistance.

Throughout this period, and especially during the 1960s and the 1970s, the Korean government launched an intensive industrial development drive that included market interventions and high import barriers in particular. Nonetheless, Korea was allowed most-favored nation (MFN) status in US markets. There was a strong and close economic partnership between the two countries, even if it was only of a vertical nature.

The 1980s saw a sudden elevation in the importance of Korean-US economic relations. In fact, economic relations surpassed security relations in importance, as evidenced by the fact that trade conflicts were allowed to threaten the security partnership. Reflecting an increase in Korea's importance as a trading partner with the United States, this new relationship coincided with Korea's emergence on the international scene as a newly industrializing economy. Korea's economic ascendancy, in turn, was a demonstration of its spectacular success with the outward-oriented development strategy, in which the government's close management of the economy played a critical role.

Trade tensions between the two nations arose in the form of four types of disputes (Bayard and Young 1989). First, the United States began to exercise contingent protection against Korean products in the form of antidumping actions, apparently with little restraint. Second, Korea became a target of US "aggressive unilateralism." With the threat of retaliatory actions under section 301 of the 1974 Trade Act, the United States began to pressure Korea to open up its domestic markets unilaterally for an ever-widening range of agricultural and industrial products as well as a number of services, in particular, financial services. Third, in a similar way, the United States began to pressure Korea to enact laws protecting intellectual property rights and to ensure enforcement. Fourth, in 1986 Korea began to experience substantial and rapidly rising current account surpluses; the emergence of these surpluses was immediately followed by US pressure on Korea to appreciate its currency and expand domestic demand to reduce, if not eliminate, them.

The Korean government accommodated most of the US requests but only after protracted negotiations and with demonstrated reluctance. As a result, retaliations were threatened and political tensions developed. These tensions peaked to a crisis level during 1988–89, when the United States introduced the 1988 Omnibus Trade and Competitiveness Act, which incorporated the so-called "super 301" provisions, and sought forceful negotiations with Korea under the act.

The emergence of Korean-US trade tensions in the 1980s may be explained in terms of three underlying factors. One is the difference in economic systems. The United States had a free market economy, while Korea had a strongly dirigiste economy, with highly regulated markets and heavily protected producers. For this reason, American firms thought they faced unfair competition vis-à-vis Korean firms in the Korean domestic markets as well as their own domestic markets. The United States would have ignored this unfair competition had Korea still lagged far behind the United States in terms of its industrial competitiveness. But as a result of its continued rapid industrial progress, the Korean economy had become too competitive to be ignored. Korea thus came to be subjected to pressure from the United States and other trading partners to "graduate" from the dirigiste and protectionist policy regimes of its earlier developmental era.

Korea could not easily accommodate such pressures to graduate. For one thing, the government was not willing to give up its earlier policy entirely because it believed that market intervention as well as infant-industry protection was still necessary in some cases. In other cases, it wanted to liberalize the market but was unable to do so because political opposition from the producers was too strong or because the bureaucracy resisted the policy directive for liberalization in order to retain its power over the market.

When the international pressure to graduate met domestic resistance, trade tensions were inevitable. Aggressive unilateralism heightened this tension.

Korean-US Economic Relations in the Early 1990s

Compared with the preceding decade, the 1990s have been thus far marked by the relative absence of a trade conflict between the two countries. With the exception of a brief flare-up in reaction to Korea's so-called austerity campaign in 1990, which addressed the sudden deterioration of the country's trade balance, there appears to have been a marked improvement in Korean-US economic relations. But often, things are not what they seem. To fully appreciate the meaning of this calm, we have to see what lies beneath it.

Three developments explain the calm that immediately followed the Korean-US bilateral trade negotiations under super 301 in 1989. First, as a result of these negotiations, Korea agreed to several measures accommodating the US demands for a level playing field: enforcement of intellectual property rights laws, a program of partial agricultural import liberalization, a commitment to graduate from the GATT Article XIX B waiver for import restrictions by 1997, and a number of measures to improve market access for industrial products, as well as those to ease restrictions on foreign direct investment.

Second, as part of its five-year program of unilateral tariff reduction that began in 1989, Korea continued to reduce its tariffs on industrial products across the board, which in turn furthered the opening of Korean markets.

Third, Korea's trade-account surpluses, which reached a peak level in 1988, began to decline in 1989 and were replaced by deficits beginning in 1990. Korea's trade account with the United States rose to a surplus of $9.6 billion in 1987 but ended up recording a deficit of about $1 billion in 1994.

It is still true that the United States continues to identify Korean trade and investment barriers to its products and firms, as it did during the early 1990s. However, two developments during this period prevented these issues from causing a major international quarrel.

One is the fact that the Uruguay Round was under way. For this reason, bilateral discussions on many thorny issues such as agriculture and some services were put on hold, pending the outcome of the round. In the end, the Uruguay Round was successfully concluded in May 1994.

The other development was the January 1992 launch, by Presidents Roh Taewoo of Korea and George Bush, of the Presidents' Economic Initiative (PEI), which was meant to be a structured dialogue to anticipate problems and develop programmed approaches for their early resolution. Under PEI, bilateral task forces were established to identify potential irritants in such areas as customs, standards, investment, and technology and to develop joint recommendations to the relevant governments—the Korean government in most of the cases—as to how to remove them.

When the PEI program concluded in June 1993, most of the identified issues remained unresolved. Still, both governments considered the program useful enough to justify a sequel. Thus, in July 1993, when Presidents Kim Young Sam and Bill Clinton met in Seoul, they agreed to follow up on the PEI with a new Dialogue for Economic Cooperation (DEC). Concluded in June 1994, the DEC addressed a number of issues ranging from investment to deregulation to competition policy and industrial cooperation; the focal topic, however, was investment. Despite its conclusion, the so-called counterpart groups are still working, and the two governments will meet at the subcabinet level in early 1995 to monitor the implementation of DEC recommendations and assess progress.

Now that the Uruguay Round is over, one major factor that has kept US aggressive unilateralism in check in recent years is no longer in place. A renewal of attention to bilateral issues is likely, and the United States will be tempted to employ aggressive unilateralism again whenever the rules of the new World Trade Organization permit it. Whether this confrontational approach and the consequent Korean-US trade tension will return depends very much on how the United States assesses the outcome of DEC.

Should the United States determine that the cooperative dialogue has been useful, the DEC is likely to continue in one form or another, largely superseding the unilateralist approach. Alternatively, should the United States determine that the cooperative dialogue has not been particularly useful, DEC is unlikely to be continued, and the tension-ridden unilateralist approach is likely to dominate. Thus, Korean-US economic relations have come to a crossroads once again, as they did during the late 1980s, and soon the United States will have to make a choice.

Confrontation and Consequences

The clues as to which path the United States will take are best found in the annual reports on Korea by the American Chamber of Commerce (AMCHAM), the US Trade Representative (USTR), and the US Treasury. They are not encouraging.

In its 1994 version of *Trade and Investment Issues*, AMCHAM Seoul exhorts the Korean government to "understand that 'foreign' is not necessarily bad" and discusses a long list of Korean barriers to US exports and investment. In the 1994 *National Trade Estimate Report On Foreign Trade Barriers*, USTR concludes a critical report on trade and investment barriers in Korea by saying that "US firms continue to report that Korea remains one of the most difficult markets in which to trade and invest." The US Treasury continues to note pervasive governmental regulation of the financial market, which prohibits its development and severely hinders foreign banking in Korea. Permeating these reports is the sense that the Korean market remains frustratingly closed to foreign goods and firms and that the Korean government fails to deliver what it promises in terms of market access and protection of foreign interests.

The PEI/DEC process attempted to address these concerns. As of now, the two governments agree that the dialogue has been a "modest success" (DEC Report 1994). However, with only "modest success," the process or its variants may not be satisfactory to the United States as a means for attacking the root problems.

In fact, the United States is already threatening unilateral actions to resolve several issues. One such issue is US firms' access to the automobile market in Korea. In October 1994, as it announced the renewal of its super 301 provisions, the United States identified Korea's restrictive auto import practices as an "area of concern." Another such issue is the Korean government's sudden decision in March 1994 to shorten the shelf-life of frozen heat-treated sausage from three months to 30 days. In response to the petition by American meat producers, the US government decided in November 1994 to initiate an investigation under section 301, and reportedly there will be more petitions for section 301 investigations of Korean markets.

Whatever the legal arguments, the two cases illustrate the protectionist stance of the Korean government. Under such circumstances, the choice to institute 301 proceedings may seem justified. For this reason, the United States will be strongly tempted to take this route in dealing with its problems of market access in Korea. At this point, however, the United States should think hard about whether the confrontational approach will work.

The trade and investment barriers to be encountered in Korea can be classified into two types. One are those that are expressly protectionist in intent. The problems the United States encountered in regard to exporting automobiles and sausages to Korea are clearly of this type. The others are those that are simply nuisance or procedural barriers contrary to the intent of the policy. Many of the problems confronting foreign investors are of this type. Deregulation for the removal of the barriers of this nature is a major component of the Korean government's five-year plan (1993–98).

The confrontational approach would not be very successful in forcing the Korean government to eliminate procedural barriers because their very presence indicates that the government has already failed to do so. An effective deregulation cannot really be forced upon Korea from the outside. It has to come from within. On the other hand, the confrontational approach in attacking protectionist policies in Korea will provoke strong resistance and is bound to be rancorous and acrimonious insofar as Koreans will think that the United States wants them to give up what they think is in the national interest.

Another problem with the confrontational approach is that it may in fact lead to a trade war. The possibility that Korea may stand up against the US trade offensive is not entirely nil as Korea's dependence on the US market continues to decline. Such a possibility would be even greater should the US trade offensive toward Korea coincide with similar offensives against Japan and China, and such actions may encourage a coordinated response among these nations of northeast Asia against the United States.

If a trade war were to break out, however, both the United States and Korea would lose in trade, with negative consequences for their domestic economies. There would also be a loss of valuable opportunities for cooperation in many other areas as well. In particular, Korea can be a very important partner, for both geographical and strategic reasons, to the United States for joint ventures in northeast Asia, including Japan and China (Young 1994). Korea is located at the center of northeast Asia, between two of the largest economies in the world, and it enjoys great cultural proximity to these two neighboring nations as well. Therefore, the United States may find it highly worthwhile to develop a partnership with Korea in trying to penetrate the domestic markets of Japan and China. A trade war would place such a partnership at risk.

Korea's Globalization Policy as a Solution

Should a trade confrontation between Korea and the United States develop, the greatest victim would be Korea itself, not only because of the damage it might inflict on Korea, but also because it would mean that Korea had failed to adjust to the new reality of worldwide globalization and to take advantage of resultant economic dynamism. This is because Korea's trade confrontation with the United States will in most cases mean that the country has failed to remove its barriers to foreign trade and investment.

Korea has to open up its economy to foreign products and firms, not simply to prevent trade confrontation, but more importantly to participate in the current globalization trend and thereby survive in it. Globalization of firms around the world poses competitive challenges for Korean firms and forces them to globalize as well. Globalization of Korean firms requires, however, that Korea open its markets to foreign trade and investment. Viewed in this light, Korea's trade policy coordination with the United States may be regarded and used as a means toward the goal of globalization, with the United States playing an instrumental role in promoting it, helping Korea promote the openness of its economy.

Many of Korea's barriers to imports and foreign investment are hidden in its regulatory maze. For this reason, it is important to recognize that effective deregulation is a sine qua non for opening the Korean economy. Accordingly, considering that the Korean government has been trying to deregulate during the past several years with limited success, it may have finally found the right approach to this task. In December 1994, the Korean government proposed downsizing itself and merged four of the economic ministries into two and reduced the number of economic officials by more than 1,000. The idea was that, with the more structurally simplified government and fewer officials in the remaining ministries, there would be less scope for unnecessary regulation. It remains to be seen how effective this downsizing will be in achieving deregulation.

Korea should correctly chart out its strategy for survival in the face of globalized competition and realize that under this strategy, it is essential to eliminate protectionism and liberalize trade and investment. Globalization renders the concept of technological independence obsolete. Instead, globalization means interdependence and requires cooperation and alliance rather than independence. Protectionism also becomes obsolete and should be replaced by effective market opening as well as effective deregulation.

Globalization as a policy, then, is to promote deregulation, trade liberalization, and investment liberalization. Needless to say, it would require other efforts, too, such as those to enhance human capital and social infrastructure. Based on this perspective, the Korean government has in fact just launched its Globalization Policy, beginning with the downsizing of government as well as a renewed campaign for deregulation.

But in order for this Globalization Policy to work, it is very important that the citizens of the country accept the premises underlying the policy. For this reason, of critical importance is a new mind-set among bureaucrats, businesspeople, journalists, workers, and the general public that accepts interdependence and cooperation, rather than independence and competition, as strategies for prosperity.

From this perspective, it seems very important for Korea to establish effective programs for public education on implications of globalization, including the need for liberalization of trade and investment. The programs should take various forms and have many components. One important component could be a School of Internationalization Studies, in which internationalized teaching staff offer one-year courses to citizens with mid-managerial positions from various walks of life.

The government may also work with schools, mass media, and nongovernmental organizations to organize various public discussions and symposia on those problems, such as trade disputes that arise in the course of internationalization and globalization.

Korean-US Economic Cooperation in the Era of Globalization

In this new era of globalization, Korea should rethink its development strategy, and both Korea and the United States should reconsider their strategies toward each other. Both should begin by considering each other as partners for globalization, and not merely as partners for bilateral trade. In particular, they should recognize the need for, and importance of, partnerships with each other in efforts to establish and maintain a competitive presence in markets all over the world and in northeast Asian countries in particular. Northeast Asia, which includes Japan, China, and Russia, is emerging as the most dynamic region in the world (Young 1994).

The two countries seem to be natural partners for alliance in penetrating the markets of northeast Asia (Krause 1994). And in the context of such an alliance, Korea will find it much easier to open up its economy to the United States. One way of establishing and promoting such an alliance is for the two countries to enter into a free trade agreement with each other (Dornbusch 1994). Thus, it is suggested here that the two countries seriously consider this option.

Once such a broader based, globally oriented partnership is formed, the United States can play an extremely important role in helping Korea make the reforms needed for its own Globalization Policy. The Korea-US free trade agreement will promote partnership between the businesses of the two countries. Such partnership will increase the confidence and international outlook of Korean businesses, which will in turn create the atmosphere in Korea for bolder moves toward deregulation and liberalization. At the same time, the United States will find Korea to be especially helpful as a partner in establishing a foothold in the competitive as well as protectionist Japan (Dornbusch 1994).

Ideas for these and other possible ventures between the two countries will require a framework for discussion and exploration. For this purpose the DEC offers a good model and should be continued. Its agenda should still include mutual market opening but should also look beyond to the countries' needs for globalization, the reforms these require, as well as the opportunities for cooperation they pose. And from this perspective, DEC might be better named the Dialogue for Cooperative Globalization (DCG).

With only a few years left before the beginning of the 21st century, Korea and the United States should rediscover each other in an entirely new light.

References

Bayard, Thomas O. and Soogil Young, eds. 1989. *Economic Relations between the United States and Korea: Conflict or Cooperation?* Washington: Institute for International Economics.

Dornbusch, Rudiger. 1994. "The United States and Korea in the Asia-Pacific Region: An American Perspective." *The Political Economy of Korea-United States Cooperation.* Washington: Institute for International Economics.

Krause, Lawrence. 1994. "US-Korean Bilateral Relations: An American Perspective." *The Political Economy of Korea-United States Cooperation*. Washington: Institute for International Economics.

Young, Soogil. 1994. "The United States and Korea in the Asia-Pacific Region: A Korean Perspective." In C. Fred Bergsten and Il SaKong, *The Political Economy of Korea-United States Cooperation*. Washington: Institute for International Economics.

III

KOREA–US COOPERATION IN THE ASIA PACIFIC

7

The Bogor Declaration and the Path Ahead

C. FRED BERGSTEN

The Bogor Declaration is the largest trade agreement in history. It is true that it has to be implemented and it is not a binding agreement. But neither was Punta del Este a binding agreement when it launched the Uruguay Round. None of these commitments to form major trade agreements are binding in a legal sense. Rather, they represent the political commitment to take a major step forward. With the Bogor Declaration, literally one-half the world's economy agreed to move to free trade and investment by a set date. That positions it to become the most sweeping trade agreement in history.

Furthermore, it is quite likely that the APEC process as launched at Bogor will produce the next major round of global trade liberalization, simply because the APEC countries, from the outset of APEC itself, have adopted the principle of open regionalism. Liberalization within APEC will likely be extended to the rest of the world, probably on a reciprocal basis. But given the fact that this region represents half the world economy, that's like the offer from the Mafia: it's an offer you can't refuse because you can't be blocked out preferentially from half the world. Assuming APEC does progress along the lines recommended in the EPG report, as implicitly adopted in the Bogor Declaration, these commitments can provide the fulcrum for the next round of global trade liberalization. Roughly speaking, that would double the ante since APEC constitutes half the world. With the impetus created by APEC liberalization bringing the other half along, there would be a strong prospect for substantial global liberalization.

C. Fred Bergsten is director of the Institute for International Economics.

There are some other major steps forward in the Bogor Declaration that may have gone unnoticed by those who haven't read the text. In addition to paving the way for new global liberalization, a second achievement was the APEC countries' commitment to accelerate implementation of the Uruguay Round. Again, half the world has committed to accelerating the implementation of liberalization already agreed so that the gains from the Uruguay Round can be realized more quickly.

Third, the Bogor Declaration strongly encourages further unilateral trade liberalization. This sounds strange in the United States, as we tend not to use this approach. But many East Asian countries do, and there is impetus for its continuation.

The APEC commitment may bolster the political dynamic for liberalization within individual Asian countries. Like the United States, each Asian country has seen a debate between a protectionist and a liberalizing faction. The liberalizing faction is always looking for outside advice, impetus, and pressure to help them win the day internally. The commitment by APEC leaders to move to free trade and investment in the area certainly strengthens the hand of the liberalizers and may therefore further intensify unilateral liberalization as well.

Fourth, the Bogor Declaration includes a standstill commitment, albeit a weak one, that commits the countries to "best endeavors" to avoid any new increases in trade barriers. Such standstill agreements have a checkered history; in the OECD, the G-7, and elsewhere there have been many, and they have not always been adhered to perfectly. Nevertheless, this agreement adds one more element to the process of liberalization.

Finally, beyond the panoply of the Bogor Declaration, the APEC ministerial statement, and other pronouncements, less spectacular but nonetheless important practical steps have been taken in the area of trade facilitation. An investment code has been agreed. Movement is occurring on customs harmonization. All of those practical building blocks further enhance the environment for achieving the trade liberalization commitment, but they are also important per se for business and trade in the region and thereby have real implications. In sum, certainly in terms of its promise but also in terms of concrete things that have been set in train, this could indeed be the biggest trade agreement in history.

A key point to keep in mind is that the target date is not as far off as is often characterized. Some of the skeptics have said that "free trade by 2020 is so far away it's never going to happen." But of the eighteen APEC member economies, only five or six are developing economies that will get until 2020 to liberalize. The great bulk of the membership is made up of either clearly industrial countries, such as the United States and Japan, or newly industrializing countries, some of which, like Singapore, have already agreed to join the fast-track group and others of which, like Korea, have acknowledged privately that they will be on that fast track and achieve their liberalization by 2010, not 2020. Putting the trade numbers together, 85 to 90 percent of the agreed liberalization is called for by 2010, not 2020, because the vast bulk of the trade is carried out by the advanced countries rather than by those on the slower track to 2020.

The category into which China falls is uncertain. Its trade is not now a large share of the total but certainly will grow. Whether 85 or 90 percent of liberalization occurs by 2010 depends largely on the course of events in China. But the bottom line is that the great bulk of trade under the Bogor commitment would be liberalized within 15 years. Compared with the North American Free Trade Agreement (NAFTA) and other traditional trade agreements—even US-Canada, much of whose tariff elimination was to occur over a 15-year period—this is not a long time horizon.

Another key point is that trade liberalization commitments have historically been realized at a pace much faster than that which the governments originally negotiated. In the Treaty of Rome, the European Community agreed on a twelve-year elimination of barriers, but it happened in seven. Australia and New Zealand coincidentally also negotiated a twelve-year free trade agreement that happened in seven. After laboriously working out those 10- to 15-year tariff elimination schedules, the United States and Canada heard from 600 companies that wanted to get rid of $8 billion of the tariffs immediately. After one year, accelerated schedules had overtaken the original ones.

What happens is that, once governments set the course and lay out the basic framework, the private sector takes over: they begin to invest on the basis of the eventual steady state, compete to get there first, and thereby accelerate the whole process. As usual, the governments have been too slow, understandably and rightly, because they worry about adjustment problems and the domestic politics thereof—but in practice liberalization happens faster. Thus, even without this acceleration, most liberalization will happen in 15 years rather than 25, and with it, liberalization will take place even more quickly.

The Potential Effects

There are only a few analyses so far of what might be the aggregate payoff of the Bogor commitments. In one such study, the Australians conclude that achievement of the Bogor targets would increase world output by about $366 billion a year by 2010. By comparison with the result from the same model, the Uruguay Round would increase world output by $112 billion a year by 2002. Thus Prime Minister Paul Keating has calculated that the APEC outcome is worth two to three times as much, for Australia at least, as the Uruguay Round. In his more recent formulations, Keating has claimed a doubling of the benefits. It is difficult to produce precise estimates at this early point, but the Australian study gives an order of magnitude.

At the Institute for International Economics, Gary Hufbauer and Jeffrey Schott are conducting a study to quantify those gains. Part of the project involves examination of the impact on individual APEC member countries, including Korea in cooperation with the Korea Institute for International Economic Policy, and Japan. Under the auspices of the Institute, a team of three leading Japanese economists produced the first comprehensive appraisal of the costs of current Japanese protection to the Japanese economy. The bottom line is that current Japanese protection is costing the Japanese consumer more than $100 billion a year. Between 2½ and 4 percent of Japan's GDP is essentially being wasted as a result of trade barriers. Something on the order of $50 billion worth of imports is kept out of Japan as a result of existing protection. For this one country alone, moving to trade liberalization would have an enormous impact both internally and on its trading partners and the world economy. Again, the preliminary estimates available on the impact of the APEC agreement suggest that it is potentially very large and the results could be extremely worthwhile.

The APEC Process

How did such a far-reaching event occur? In early 1993, no one would have predicted the Bogor result. Certainly no one would have done so before the Seattle summit, which, to the enormous credit of President Clinton, launched the process in a really intense and extended way later in late 1993. But even after Seattle, it would have been hard to foresee that the leaders would sit down as they did at Bogor and declare themselves ready to eliminate all their barriers to trade and investment, even over a long period.

The first key to this success was the elevation of the issue to the political level. It was up to the heads of state to act—not ministers, officials, or bureaucrats—and the leaders did lead. Without that political step, this outcome would not have been possible.

The APEC summit process has now become institutionalized. The Japanese are preparing for the Osaka summit, the Philippines will do it the following year, and Canada the year after that. In 1998, the chair goes to Malaysia. It will be very interesting to see if Prime Minister Mahathir (or his successor by that time) decides to continue the summit process. My suspicion is the inclination to host the summit will be great even in those quarters and the process will continue. But at least for the first four or five years of the evolving APEC process, leadership came from the top. Incidentally, within the United States both parties share the credit for this leadership. Ideas that evolved toward the end of the Bush administration were carried over and expanded in the first year of the Clinton administration. APEC has a distinctly bipartisan background here.

A crucial element in 1995 was the Indonesian lead, which was important because it represented leadership by an Asian developing country. No one could argue that the Bogor Declaration was foisted on Asia or on poorer countries by the Americans or anybody pursuing hegemonic pretensions. It was led from the heart of ASEAN and Southeast Asia itself, by President Suharto in particular.

President Suharto made a speech in August 1993—one month after he had discussed APEC summitry for the first time with President Clinton and three months before the Seattle summit—in which he said very explicitly that Indonesia would be taking the chair of APEC in 1994 and would give it a forceful lead. Clearly, he was already thinking along these lines more than a year before the Bogor summit. Indonesia chaired and led the summit process at APEC in 1995 at least as effectively as any G-7 country, including the United States, has ever led the G-7 summit process. The Indonesians did a superb job.

The United States has also played a major role. In 1995 in particular, it very skillfully played a supportive rather than commanding role, thereby avoiding charges that it alone was driving the process and thus enabling the process to succeed.

Korea has also played a key role. President Kim was an important leader at both Blake Island and Bogor. Earlier on, Korea fashioned the formula that permitted entry of China, Hong Kong, and Taiwan in 1991 and thus made possible all that has followed. The close cooperation between the United States and Korea that has marked the APEC process throughout its history demonstrates that industrialized and developing countries can collaborate effectively in this context.

The Eminent Persons Group probably had a role as well. The EPG report did in fact, to use Suharto's words, provide a point of reference for those who wanted to move energetically. The whole idea for the EPG was to create a body outside governments and bureaucracies to provide a vision. The group did so and then the governments followed up by endorsing it, working with it, and establishing it as the basis for progress.

The group's members, all of whom were appointed by governments but acted as individuals, were able to forge compromises on several key issues. On the issue of unilateral versus negotiated liberalization, on the global versus regional aspects of the whole strategy, and on extending the benefits to nonmembers conditionally or unconditionally, the EPG worked out balanced agreements that comprehended different viewpoints. The EPG both demonstrated that such an outcome was possible and provided a substantive basis for governments with different views on these issues to sign on to the consensus without fear that some of their own policy preferences would be undermined or cut off at the outset.

Perhaps the most important example was the EPG's four-part formula for open regionalism. We carefully defined it so as to permit individual countries, if they wished, to extend the benefits of APEC liberalization to nonmembers on an unconditional basis but also called for the group as a whole to generalize the benefits on a reciprocal basis. The Indonesians, in their interpretation of the Bogor Declaration (which they drafted), say they intended to include all elements of that formula so that the whole system could proceed as suggested in the EPG report.

One thing the APEC members did at Bogor against the recommendation of the EPG was to continue the EPG. We recommended that we be permitted to declare victory and go home. The leaders instead requested that the EPG monitor the progress of the implementation of the declaration, make recommendations for further steps, and look particularly at the relationship between APEC and the subregional agreements such as NAFTA. So we continued in existence for another year.

Another key element of the process was the Pacific Business Forum that the leaders agreed in Seattle, consisting of two businessmen from each of the 18 countries. The PBF presented a report in mid-October, which was very consistent with the EPG on the broad policy issues but went much beyond it, very thoughtfully and creatively, on the business facilitation issues. The PBF provided another base of political support to the process—a point of reference, as the Indonesians said—as well as the momentum to develop the final outcome at Bogor.

What's Next?

The crucial question now, of course, is what happens next? *Will* it happen? Will it be implemented? There are many skeptics and much doubt, and certainly several remaining questions.

One has to say at the outset that there are going to be setbacks. The history of European integration, to put it mildly, has not been a straight line. The European Defense Community failed before the Community itself ever got going. The British opted out of the EEC at an early stage. DeGaulle vetoed it for several years. The Maastricht Treaty and the European Monetary System (EMS) raise problems now. In appraising the evolution of APEC, therefore, one should not be discouraged nor give up on it if there are setbacks—especially in the early going.

Malaysia should pose no special cause for alarm, despite its reservations. First, Malaysia accounts for only 0.2 percent of the output of APEC. (All of ASEAN, in fact, accounts for only 3 percent of the output of APEC. It includes six countries, but given the size of the economies, one cannot give it undue weight.) In any event, if you look at the reservations that Prime Minister Mahathir published the day after Bogor, they are not very startling. Some simply state the obvious: that Bogor is a nonbinding agreement and that liberalization in APEC should be GATT-consistent. Some of Mahathir's statements endorse ideas in the EPG report: that individual countries can extend their liberalization on an unconditional basis and that countries may proceed unilaterally rather than through negotiations. I don't regard any of that as a big problem.

There are three or four major issues to be worked out. One is the allocation of countries as between the two categories: the fast track to liberalize by 2010 and the slower track by 2020. President Suharto in his press conference after Bogor counted five countries that are clearly in the industrial category: the United States, Canada, Japan, Australia, and New Zealand. Subsequently, the prime minister of Singapore publicly volunteered to join the fast track. Private discussions both at Bogor, as I understand it, and subsequently indicated that Korea (and certainly the other newly industrializing economies, Taiwan and Hong Kong) would be on the fast track. It is on this basis that I arrive at a figure of 85 percent of APEC trade being liberalized by 2010—the great bulk of it by any calculation.

China will be an issue. In this context, it is important to wait and see how Chinese development evolves and how its entry into the World Trade Organization (WTO) works out. When actual liberalization begins to kick in (around the year 2000 in the EPG formula, though that has not been agreed yet), China can be placed in the appropriate category and evaluated then.

The difference in income among the countries within APEC is much greater than the gap between NAFTA's members. In NAFTA, the per capita income gap between wealthiest and poorest was 8:1 or 10:1. In APEC, the gap is 30:1. Japan's per capita income at early 1995 market exchange rates is $30,000 or more. The United States' is about $23,000. On most calculations, China is about $1,000, and Indonesia is about $700. The justification for a slower liberalization track for those countries is of course the vast disparity in standards of living and the like. But the gains to the United States and all the industrialized countries on the fast track are still so enormous that they certainly should pursue the opportunity.

Another question is coverage. Some countries in the group were already nervous about agriculture. Some were nervous about investment. Mahathir's reservations led him to say that APEC should only liberalize "substantially" all trade; that's consistent with GATT Article 24, of course, but it's not as good as the leaders promised when they included all trade without exceptions. That issue obviously will have to be worked out with the usual debate about exclusions that one gets in any trade negotiation. There may have to be different time paths for very sensitive sectors, but certainly there should be a major effort to limit or even avoid making exceptions.

Even more complicated will be extension of liberalization to primarily domestic policy measures of the type that are particularly acute in the current US negotiations with Japan. The EPG report was very clear that those have to be included. The APEC ministerial declaration enumerated a number of them as already being on the agenda, with others to be discussed. This will be difficult and tricky, too, but to be successful, one clearly has to go beyond border measures.

A third issue is the treatment of nonmembers. Are nonmembers to be given automatic access to the APEC liberalization, as some in APEC would have it? Or should they simply be offered the opportunity to achieve access to the APEC market on a reciprocal basis? As I mentioned before, the EPG report suggested a four-part formula that included both options. The Indonesians, at least, interpret the Bogor Declaration as encompassing that formula. It has, however, not been explicitly agreed, and that too has to be worked out.

All this raises a critical process question, and all interested parties should apply themselves to answering it: what is the best process through which a political commitment of such a far-reaching nature can now be implemented? The traditional approach would be to sit down in face-to-face negotiations over the major issues: timing, duration, treatment of outsiders, and the like. That may in fact be the best way.

But an alternative would be for individual member countries of APEC to come forward with basically unilateral offers, saying, "We've made the political commitment, and here's how we intend to do it." Countries could lay out their own timetables and their ideas of what the coverage would be, what the treatment of outsiders would be, and so on. If four or five of the most forthcoming members of the organization came forward with those ideas, with implementation contingent on what everybody else did at the end of the day, then they would have a very good chance of leading the process. Peer pressure and demonstration effects could produce emulation by other members that could move them in a similarly aggressive direction on all of these variables. The face-to-face negotiation on the principles at this point might not yield such a positive outcome. There might be foot dragging. So I think consideration should be given to that more heterodox approach. This approach will undoubtedly play a pivotal role in cooperation between the United States and Korea.

The outcome at Bogor was substantial. It offers enormous promise. For the reasons suggested above, I believe it will have an enormous effect. As we look back at Bogor and Seattle from five or ten or fifteen years out, it will turn out that these were seminal events in the course of world trade policy and perhaps in the broader international arena as well.

APEC is central to the future agenda of relations between Korea and the United States. It in fact represents a way to achieve free trade between both countries that is far superior to a bilateral free trade agreement, or Korean accession to NAFTA, because it avoids the problem of preferential treatment and discrimination against neighbors. There will be a bigger payoff for both countries from a successful APEC, and they should make every effort to welcome it.

8

Cooperation between the United States and Korea

JANG-HEE YOO AND TAEHO BARK

A wide range of sectors within the national economies of the world are rapidly integrating as the global economy emerges. Goods and services, once only traded between and among isolated national economies, are now traded across all national borders. Multinational corporations are becoming the principle mechanism through which investment capital is allocated and the location of production is determined. Globalization will be accelerated by strict enforcement of multilateral rules and regulations by the World Trade Organization (WTO), which has replaced the General Agreement on Tariffs and Trade (GATT) as a mechanism to guide and oversee world trade relations.

Rising regionalism threatens to reverse or counteract the transnational consolidation trend. Many have suggested that today's world economy will evolve into a tripolar system of economic blocs, consisting of Europe, North and South America, and East Asia.[1] Such polarization would undoubtedly produce friction among individual blocs of nations as they compete for larger shares of the economic pie.

Notwithstanding rising regionalism, the emergence of the Asia Pacific Economic Cooperation (APEC) forum suggests that the fragmentation of the world economy into three economic blocs can be avoided. Recently, the United States has shown a keen interest in APEC as a means of fulfilling its economic agenda, as well as expediting global multilateralism.

Jang-Hee Yoo and Taeho Bark are, respectively, president and vice president of the Korea Institute for International Economic Policy (KIEP), Seoul.

1. For a good summary of discussions on the prospects of regionalization, see Young (1992).

Japan's political leadership has also embraced the spirit of partnership in the Asia-Pacific region. Beyond these two major economies, APEC also includes the world's most dynamic economies, such as the newly industrializing Asian economies, ASEAN, and China.[2] Considering Asia's growth potential and human capital resources, a bipolar system consisting of Europe and the Asia Pacific, rather than a tripartite division, is becoming more likely.

Coupled with the emergence of the WTO, the bipolarization of the world economy may actually promote an open multilateral trading system, as the European Union and APEC each compete to liberalize faster than the other. Despite potential problems, the spirit of multilateralism will eventually prevail as the basis of the future international economic order and surmount regional differences, but only if both the European Union and APEC support sound and constructive regionalism.

Viability of the European Union and APEC

There are a number of characteristics that make the European Union and APEC viable as complementary regional trade arrangements. First, a regional trade arrangement must express joint objectives. Both the European Union and APEC were established to exploit commonalities through achievement of economic integration in the case of the European Union, and regional trade liberalization and development cooperation in the case of APEC.[3]

Second, one should not understate the importance of forces that bind countries participating in regional arrangements—for example, European homogeneity has made EU integration possible. With the establishment of the European Union, member countries have ceded significant national sovereignty over economic affairs to regional bodies such as the European Commission and the European Court of Justice. In addition, member countries will have to work out a mechanism to make a common fiscal and monetary policy.

While EU integration has been based on European homogeneity, APEC's common denominators are the dynamism and complementarities within the region. Economic dynamism stems from, among other things, the recent revival of self-identity among the member countries, many of

---

2. There are 18 member economies in APEC: the United States, Canada, Chile, Mexico, Japan, Australia, New Zealand, Papua New Guinea, Asian NIEs (South Korea, Taiwan, Hong Kong, and Singapore), and ASEAN (Indonesia, Malaysia, Philippines, Thailand, Brunei Darussalam).

3. Given the diverse nature of the APEC economies and for all member economies to derive the maximum benefits, it is desirable that trade liberalization be balanced by developing cooperation.

whom have suffered under the hegemony of neighboring superpowers. Since the United States, China, and Japan are still viewed as potential threats, smaller countries in the region would greatly welcome a system that encompasses these nations as contributing members. While homogeneity has driven EC countries to continue cooperation in the Asia-Pacific region, historical tensions with larger powers may drive smaller countries in the region to cooperate with each other and work collectively as a single economic entity.[4]

The size and scale of the regional arrangement, both in terms of population and economic output, is another critical element for sustaining regional blocs. Regional arrangements of sufficient size can command the international community's attention and thus take part in shaping the world economic order. The European Union and APEC are sufficiently large. The European Economic Area (EEA), consisting of the original twelve EC member states and six countries of the European Free Trade Association (EFTA), has emerged as the largest single market in the world, accounting for roughly 41 percent of world trade. The combined GDP of EEA member states is more than $6 trillion, and its population is roughly 340 million (table 1). APEC is of sufficient size in terms of GDP and population to compete with the EEA; thus its voice will be heard in the world community.

Finally, another key factor is the presence of a stabilizing leader country that can drive regional cooperation. The internal stability of the European Union and APEC can be attributed to Germany's role in the European Union and the United States' in APEC. If these stabilizing forces are missing, regional arrangements are often unsustainable.

APEC's Vision: Looking Beyond the WTO

The Asia Pacific is economically the world's most dynamic region. The region produces over half of the world's output and accounts for a large share of world trade. If the current high economic growth of the region continues into the 21st century, the region will possess two-thirds of world output; these numbers suggest that the region may become the center of the world economy. From a population standpoint, more people live in the Asia-Pacific region than in any other part of the world.

Rapid economic growth in the Asia Pacific would not have been pos-

---

4. In comparison with other APEC member economies, ASEAN countries tend to maintain a concerted voice on various policy initiatives in APEC. ASEAN, at the inception of APEC, expressed its views on the institutional questions and maintained that the basic principles for APEC should be "in any enhanced Asia-Pacific economic cooperation, ASEAN's identity and cohesion should be preserved and its cooperative relations with its dialogue partners and with other third countries should not be diluted" (Kim 1990).

Table 1 Share of world output and trade by region, 1970–2010

	APEC[a]	EU	Rest of world	Total
World output				
1970				
Billions of dollars	1,528.5	713.5	304.1	2,546.1
Share of total	60.0	28.0	12.0	
1990				
Billions of dollars	10,835.5	6,183.9	2,381.2	19,400.6
Share of total	55.9	31.9	12.2	
Average 2000–10				
Billions of dollars	29,476	13,107	7,990	50,573
Share of total	58.3	25.9	15.8	
World trade				
1971				
Billions of dollars	297.7	376.3	117.7	791.7
Share of total	37.6	25.9	15.8	
1990				
Billions of dollars	3,856.1	3,498.1	1,190.2	8,544.4
Share of total	45.1	41.0	13.9	
Average 2000–10				
Billions of dollars	14,186	8,835	3,487	26,508
Share of total	53.5	33.3	13.2	

a. Excluding Brunei and Papua New Guinea.

Source: DRI/McGraw-Hill, *World Markets Executive Overview*, Second Quarter 1994.

sible without a high level of regional economic interdependence, which has been sustained for more than 20 years through active trade and investment flows. By 1990 the intraregional share of exports of most Asia-Pacific economies exceeded 60 percent, and that share has continued to increase (table 2). Increasing rates of foreign direct investment within the region also indicate growing economic interdependence. Japan and the United States have supplied a large share of the foreign capital in the region's developing economies, while the Asian NIEs have recently emerged as an important source of capital for the region's other developing economies (table 3).

Moreover, countries in the Asia-Pacific region have come to recognize that close cooperation and coordination is essential to sustaining the region's economic growth. They therefore support an institutional arrangement to strengthen intraregional relationships.[5]

---

5. Since the fifth APEC ministerial meeting in Seattle, APEC made substantial progress in institutionalization. First of all, President Clinton called for the first APEC summit in Seattle. Indonesian President Suharto convened the second one, which was followed by the third in November 1995 in Osaka, Japan. Second, a Committee on Trade and Investment (CTI) was established "to create a coherent APEC objective and voice on global trade and investment issues and increase cooperation among members on key issues." Third, an Economic Committee (EC) had its inaugural meeting in Fukuoka on 8–9 February 1995 to "strengthen APEC's capability in the analysis of long-term macroeconomic trends and studies of microeconomic issues" (APEC 1995).

Table 2 Intraregional trade dependence, 1970 and 1990
(export shares)

Exporting region	APEC	EU	Rest of world
APEC			
1970	54.21	22.04	23.75
1990	65.43	17.97	16.60
EU			
1970	14.61	53.10	32.29
1990	13.27	55.77	30.96
Rest of world			
1970	31.18	24.86	43.96
1990	21.30	26.26	52.44

Source: C. Fred Bergsten and Marcus Noland, eds., 1992, *Pacific Dynamism and the International Economic System* (Washington: Institute for International Economics).

The multilateral free trade system has been essential to rapid economic growth, as was demonstrated by the experience of the Asia-Pacific countries. However, increased protectionism, escalation of regionalism (particularly the inward-looking regionalism of the European Union), and bilateral trade disputes have jeopardized the growth of the global trade system, heightening the need for an open regional bloc that is consistent with an open multilateral trading system.

APEC was established with the ultimate goal of strengthening the open multilateral trade system, which is predicated on nondiscriminatory policies. APEC member states thus rely on open regionalism in their regional trade arrangement—avoiding harm to nonmember countries and instead inviting them to participate in liberalization measures.[6]

The Uruguay Round negotiations illustrate how difficult it is to strike a deal when so many agents negotiate for liberalization. APEC intended to avoid such difficulties by first striking a mutually beneficial deal among a smaller subset of countries. This incremental approach allows similarly situated economies to act first and then applies the momentum from the initial agreement toward expanding the process to the rest of the world.

---

6. The concept of open regionalism has been widely discussed among policy analysts since the early 1980s as an alternative mode of regional economic cooperation to replace the old-style regionalism in the mode of the European Union and NAFTA. According to the definition of Drysdale (1992), open regionalism envisages a nonexclusive and nondiscriminatory regional economic regime in which each country pursues liberalization in its own interest and becomes the principal beneficiary of its own liberalization. Regional economic integration along this line is led by the market mechanism, rather than being forced by mutually binding trade, and individual economies choose the pace of liberalization that suits their own economic and political conditions. Proponents of this idea claim that recent economic integration and growth in the Western Pacific well reflects the idea of open regionalism.

Table 3 Foreign direct investment flows, 1980–91 (millions of dollars)

Regions receiving investment	Year	US & Canada		Western Pacific area						APEC
		Total	US only	Total	Japan	China	NIEs 4	ASEAN 4	Oceania	
US & Canada	1980	3,516	238	1,188	978	2	224	-16	65	4,769
	1985	-1,231	-2,142	3,564	3,473	1	70	20	1,229	3,562
	1991	1,473	2,797	6,174	5,542	0	647	-15	181	7,828
Western Pacific area	1980	1,038	1,037	763	476	5	273	9	7	1,808
	1985	1,988	1,977	2,902	1,299	28	1,530	45	59	4,949
	1991	3,802	3,035	11,331	4,517	194	6,437	183	385	15,518
Japan	1980	111	111	0	—	n.a.	n.a.	n.a.	-1	110
	1985	514	514	0	—	n.a.	n.a.	n.a.	n.a.	514
	1991	647	-89	8	—	-1	9	n.a.	3	658
China	1980	n.a.	n.a.	0	n.a.	—	n.a.	n.a.	n.a.	n.a.
	1985	366	357	1,293	315	—	966	12	14	1,673
	1991	334	323	3,026	533	—	2,463	30	16	3,376
NIEs 4	1980	742	742	416	263	0	145	8	0	1,158
	1985	924	923	869	779	22	50	18	1	1,794
	1991	2,047	2,047	2,088	1,811	130	131	16	177	4,312
ASEAN	1980	185	184	347	213	5	128	1	8	540
	1985	184	183	740	205	6	514	15	44	968
	1991	774	754	6,209	2,173	65	3,834	137	189	7,172
Oceania	1980	1,049	950	522	364	0	0	158	97	1,668
	1985	697	692	397	767	0	0	-370	95	1,189
	1991	n.a.	n.a.	n.a.	n.a.	n.a.	n.a.	n.a.	n.a.	n.a.
APEC total	1980	5,603	2,225	2,473	1,818	7	497	151	169	8,245
	1985	1,454	527	6,863	5,539	29	1,600	-305	1,383	9,700
	1991	5,275	5,832	17,505	10,059	194	7,084	168	566	23,346

n.a. = not available.

Source: "Vision for the Economy of the Asia-Pacific Region in the Year 2000 and Tasks Ahead," APEC Ad Hoc Economic Group Meeting (Tokyo), 1992.

In its second report, the Eminent Persons Group (EPG) proposed that APEC achieve free and open trade by the year 2020 by pursuing a "WTO-Plus" agenda.[7] The EPG recommended maximum unilateral liberalization of trade and investment barriers by all APEC member countries (APEC 1994, 30). According to this line of thinking, voluntary liberalization on the part of member countries would have spillover effects, encouraging other countries to liberalize further. Unilateral liberalization on the part of individual member countries in the region would then contribute to the expansion of trade, investment, and growth throughout the entire region.

Second, all APEC liberalization would be implemented in accordance with open regionalism.[8] A regional commitment to reduce trade barriers among APEC member states would also apply to nonmember states. This notion goes well beyond the GATT requirement that new regional trade arrangements avoid introducing any additional barriers against nonmember countries at their outset. To avoid any free-rider problems associated with the offering of regionwide liberalization to nonmember states, APEC would follow a "racheting-up" approach based on the conditional most-favored nation (MFN) principle. Considering the economic power of APEC, such an offer would give nonmember countries an incentive to reduce trade barriers, thereby triggering full-scale global liberalization.

Third, bilateral trade disputes, particularly among the largest economies of the region, have been a major concern of APEC member countries. The recent breakdown of the US-Japan Framework Talks suggests that these two major players in the region still disagree on various trade issues. The ill-managed relationship between the two economies and the aggravated conflicts arising from it may spill over to other member states and thus endanger the integrity of APEC. Consequently, APEC should promote effective dispute mediation services among the leading economies of the region.

---

7. The APEC Eminent Persons Group (EPG), comprising nongovernmental eminent persons from the region, was established by a decision at the fourth APEC ministerial, held at Bangkok in 1992. The EPG was asked to assess regional trade in the medium term, identifying constraints affecting the growth of regional trade and making policy recommendations for the institutional changes required to expand and liberalize trade.

8. The innovation of the second EPG report lies in the EPG's definition of open regionalism. According to the traditional concept of open regionalism, all liberalization agreed upon by APEC member economies should be extended to nonmembers on an unconditional MFN basis. However, this approach would induce a "free rider" problem—that is, the nonmember countries would not have any incentive to liberalize their own economies in return for benefits provided by member countries. In this regard, the EPG recommended that APEC extend its liberalization on a conditional MFN basis to nonmembers that are willing to accept obligations similar to those imposed upon the member countries. Considering the economic power of APEC, represented by its sizable market and immense growth potential, such an offer by APEC as a group would induce nonmember countries to reduce their trade barriers, thereby triggering full-scale global liberalization.

Although a dispute settlement system has existed for many years under the GATT, it has been largely ineffective. A country found to violate multilateral rules could veto the dispute settlement panel's orders for corrective actions. The Uruguay Round, however, included a strengthened dispute settlement mechanism, which went into effect with the establishment of the WTO. The WTO procedures will be binding and will not be subject to the same excessive delays as was the GATT procedure. Given this strengthened device for settling trade conflicts under the WTO, APEC mediation services have been designed to cover issues not covered by the WTO, as well as issues that could be resolved within the region through dialogues and discussions without resorting to a binding mechanism.

The Bogor Declaration and Future Tasks

At the 1994 meeting in Indonesia, APEC leaders adopted the Bogor Declaration, which calls for the strengthening of the current scheme of cooperation in APEC, transforming it from a loose, informal consultative forum into a substantial organization that will build a program of future trade and investment liberalization in the Asia Pacific (APEC 1995, 5).

The Bogor Declaration defines the timetable for regional trade and investment liberalization. In the declaration, APEC leaders committed to free and open trade and investment in the Asia Pacific by 2020. The pace of liberalization agreed upon differs for individual APEC member states, taking into account varying levels of economic development. Developed member states are committed to liberalization by the end of 2010, while the developing member countries are required to achieve this goal by no later than 2020.

The Bogor Declaration also supports the goal of sustained growth of the region's developing economies, recognizing that "the Asia Pacific industrialized economies will provide opportunities for developing economies to increase further their economic growth and their level of development" (APEC 1995). Accordingly, technology transfer and capital investment from the region's developed economies to the developing economies will be encouraged. Developed countries' efforts in this area will facilitate APEC's progress toward free and open trade in the Asia Pacific.

The declaration also discusses the strengthening of the open multilateral trading system and intensified development cooperation. Recognizing that an open multilateral trading system drives dynamic growth in the region, APEC leaders affirmed active participation in the WTO system and agreed to assume a leadership role. To achieve sustainable and balanced growth among APEC member countries, APEC leaders also emphasized the development of trade facilitation programs such as investment in human capital and industrial infrastructure. Foreign direct investment on the part of the private sector has played a crucial role in the economic progress of the region. Accordingly, APEC leaders called for private-sector leadership in trade facilitation.

Given that the political will to achieve free and open trade and investment in the Asia Pacific exists, individual APEC member countries need to ready themselves by preparing blueprints for liberalization. Important details, including the scale and scope of liberalization, timetables, and reference to MFN principles in extending regionwide liberalization to nonmember countries were not included in the Bogor Declaration.

The Asia-Pacific countries are remarkably diverse in cultural background, legal and political structures, and level of economic development. This diversity creates enormous opportunities for future expansion of mutually beneficial trade and investment. It may also, however, threaten the stability of APEC. Consequently, the regional approach to liberalization in the Asia Pacific requires the harmonization of developed and developing economies' views. To the extent that liberalization increases developed member states' access to the domestic markets of the region's developing economies, developing countries need to be compensated by receiving technology transfer and the capital needed to construct their industrial infrastructure.

US-Korean Cooperation within APEC

Notwithstanding the determination and convictions of APEC leaders, skeptics still have reservations about the future development of APEC. Many point out that the region's developing economies view APEC as a scheme of the region's developed economies to force the opening of their markets. The success of the US-Korean economic relationship for the past five decades, however, demonstrates that APEC can evolve into a regional cooperative body whereby both developed and developing economies can prosper.

Over the past five decades, the Korean economy has become a model for other developing economies. There are several reasons for Korea's remarkable economic performance. The support of the United States, particularly at the initial stage of economic development, was critical to jump-starting the growth of the Korean economy. Sometimes propelled by US economic assistance and sometimes through US political pressure, Korea was able to overcome a shortage of capital, infrastructure, and resources, an unstable political and social environment, and a closed and nationalistic market structure. The United States provided Korea with financial aid and granted Korean exporters broad access to the US market in order to encourage economic growth. Thus, current developing APEC members can benefit from trading with the developed APEC members in a liberalized trade environment.

The United States has also benefited greatly from its stable and close relationship with Korea. Korea's rapid economic growth has created one of the most important US export markets. Korea is the United States' second largest economic partner among Asian countries, immediately following Japan, with respect to trade and investment.

The United States and Korea therefore need to make concerted efforts to convince the region's developing countries that APEC can evolve into a workable framework in which the prosperity of all members is promoted, following the US-Korea example. Empirical studies show that the US-Korean economic relationship over the past five decades has been a "win-win" relationship for both sides. Moreover, it is also important to emphasize Korea's efforts to liberalize voluntarily. In recent years, Korea, with the realization that economic prosperity will no longer be achieved without liberalization, has committed itself to the liberalization of the domestic economy in such key areas as the finance and retail sectors.

The heterogeneity of the Asia-Pacific region is another factor skeptics frequently cite for uncertainty concerning APEC's viability. Many have claimed that it is extremely difficult to find a commonality of interests in the Asia Pacific, which features great disparities in terms of economic systems, practices, and values. However, the US-Korean experience suggests that heterogeneity does not preclude mutually advantageous development.

Another example suggesting that heterogeneity is not an insurmountable obstacle is the successful expansion of trade and investment between the United States and Latin American countries. Moreover, the United States and Latin America have moved toward a Free Trade Area of the Americas. Similar evidence is found in the Korean case. Notwithstanding the different economic systems and environments, Korea has maintained an intimate economic partnership with Russia and China. Accordingly, the United States and Korea can make a strong case before the other members of APEC that heterogeneity need not be an obstacle.

There are many other areas in which close US-Korean cooperation will be necessary to support the future development of APEC. Over the past several years, the bilateral trade relationship has improved significantly through continuous dialogue and consultation. Nonetheless, a number of unresolved trade issues remain. They include the liberalization of Korea's automobile and meat markets, the extension by Korea of intellectual property rights, and various US unilateral actions, such as "super 301" trade sanctions, as well as US social security tax exemptions, mutual recognition of safety inspections, and the abuse of antidumping provisions. These disputes need to be resolved promptly, thereby showing other APEC member countries that the two countries are committed to cooperation.

Recently, both the United States and Korea have experienced considerable difficulties in their domestic economies due to weakening industrial competitiveness in certain sectors. For instance, Korean products have been losing competitiveness in the export market as a result of wage increases beyond what labor productivity improvements can support, a shortage of capital for infrastructure projects, inadequate research and development investment, and overheated growth of the service sector. US-Korean industrial cooperation, which exploits the respective strengths of each country—that is, Korea's manufacturing base and the advanced technology of the United States—will help improve international competitiveness of both. Such cooperation will be particularly useful in reducing production costs, improving the product quality, and shortening the development time for new products. More importantly, industrial cooperation will demonstrate that there are many areas in which developed and developing economies, despite their differences, can pursue mutual prosperity.

In addition to industrial cooperation, technological interactions will also emerge as a key issue in shaping the future economic relationship between the United States and Korea. Currently, many industrialized countries are seeking to collaborate on technology development in order to survive intensifying competition. Falling behind this trend toward cooperative ventures would seriously damage the Korean economy, which has committed to restructuring its economy to embrace technology-oriented industries. In particular, now that technology transfer is costly and difficult, not being included in technology collaborations would make it extremely difficult for Korea to gain access to the advanced technology essential for further economic growth.

Given its dominant role in virtually all areas of the global economy, some claim that the United States has little incentive to engage in technological cooperation with Korea. However, such a claim is unjustified. The United States would also benefit greatly from joint technology ventures with Korea. For example, the United States could use Korea, with its growth potential and geographical location, as a platform for US advancement into other parts of Asia, and Korea is attractive to many US firms as a potential market as well. As with industrial cooperation, technological cooperation between the United States and Korea will also demonstrate a commonality of interest between these two very different economies.

Cooperative research on the part of the two countries will also be very important. As the APEC system evolves, there will be both trade creation and trade diversion in several industries and sectors. The World Bank has recently estimated that trade and investment liberalization in East Asia would bring about gains of $100 billion annually. Academics of the two countries should develop models to better explain the potential effects of APEC initiatives. Joint research projects on issues related to APEC, currently being undertaken by the Korea Institute for International Economic Policy and the Institute for International Economics, are good examples of such efforts.

Finally, the United States and Korea should jointly explore the possibility of inviting new members into APEC after 1996, as some of the countries in the region will soon be ready to join the system. In particular, both countries ought to consider various means of inducing North Korea to join APEC and other international organizations.

Concluding Remarks

Toward the end of this century, a dramatically different world economic order based on multilateral principles will emerge. There are two central reasons supporting this view. First and most obvious, a bright outlook for global free trade stems from the successful conclusion of the Uruguay Round. Undoubtedly, GATT has contributed to the growth of the world economy during the postwar period. However, there have also been widespread derogations from multilateral principles, which elicited comprehensive rescue efforts in Uruguay in 1986. With almost all of the unpleasant disagreements that surfaced during the negotiation resolved, the world economy is now poised to take a significant step toward global free trade under the stewardship of the WTO.

Another reason for optimism lies in APEC. The impressive economic growth of the Asia-Pacific region was largely made possible by the free trade system. This implies that a worldwide open trade system is vital to the region's continued economic growth. Over the past few years, the Asia-Pacific region has put a great deal of effort into forming a freer and more liberalized trade regime in the form of APEC. Although some subregional groups such as the North American Free Trade Agreement and the ASEAN Free Trade Agreement have tended to develop into inward-looking economic blocs, APEC will be able to incorporate all of these partial solutions, leading eventually to the global optimum for free trade.

Despite the grounds for optimism, there remains a great deal of uncertainty concerning APEC. APEC skeptics have raised heterogeneity as an insurmountable constraint on cooperation in the Asia-Pacific region, claiming that the region's inherent structural differences and cultural diversity will make substantial cooperation unlikely. The fear on the part of some developing member states that the developed countries will selfishly use APEC as a device to increase their access to foreign markets is another factor raised by skeptics.

Joint leadership by the United States and Korea will be essential for the successful development of APEC, since the two countries are prime examples of how such problems can easily be surmounted with a view toward mutual prosperity. Before US-Korean relations can serve as a model for the region, however, there are a multitude of differences that both countries must confront, including the resolution of bilateral trade disputes, balanced trade expansion, and industrial and technological cooperation. However, these issues can be easily resolved with continuous dialogue and consultations.

References

Asia Pacific Economic Cooperation (APEC). 1993. *A Vision for APEC: Towards an Asia Pacific Economic Community.* Report of the Eminent Persons Group to APEC Ministers. Singapore: APEC Secretariat.

Asia Pacific Economic Cooperation (APEC). 1994. *Achieving the APEC Vision: Free and Open Trade in the Asia Pacific.* Second Report of the Eminent Persons Group. Singapore: APEC Secretariat.

Asia Pacific Economic Cooperation (APEC). 1995. "APEC Economic Leaders' Declaration of Common Resolve." Selected APEC Documents (February).

Drysdale, Peter. 1992. "The Pacific: An Application of a General Theory of Economic Integration." Proceedings of PAFTAD 20, Pacific Dynamism and the International Economic System. Washington: Institute for International Economics.

Kim, Chungsoo. 1990. "Regional Economic Cooperation Bodies in the Asia-Pacific: Working Mechanism and Linkages." In Jang-Won Suh and Jae-Bong Ro, *Seminar Proceedings, Asia-Pacific Economic Cooperation: The Way Ahead.* Seoul: Korea Institute for International Economic Policy.

Korea Institute for International Economic Policy (KIEP). 1991. *Northeast Asian Economic Cooperation: Perspectives and Challenges.* Proceedings of papers presented at a forum hosted by KIEP. Seoul.

Korea Institute for International Economic Policy (KIEP). 1994. *1994 World Economic Forecast and Korea's International Economic Policy.* Policy Material #94-01 (in Korean). Seoul.

Korea Institute for International Economic Policy (KIEP) and Korea Pacific Economic Cooperation (KOPEC). 1993. *New Directions for Asia Pacific Economic Cooperation.* Policy Report #93-33 (in Korean). Seoul.

Ro, Jae-Bong. 1993. *Deepening Regionalism and Korea's Choice.* Policy Material #93-12, Korea Institute for International Economic Policy (in Korean).

APPENDICES

Importance of the US-Korean Alliance

PETER TARNOFF

The Korea–United States Twenty-First Century Council occupies an important place in the thick fabric of our countries' relations. For those who have participated in its discussions, the usefulness of the Council's yearly meetings is already evident. For the benefit of the rest, perhaps I might take a few moments to describe why it is so important for top leaders in the United States and South Korea to stay in close touch and work together on common concerns and goals.

The Council convenes a unique cross-section of distinguished Koreans and Americans. Government officials and former policymakers who still actively give counsel to their governments are involved, as are business executives at the top of their professions and journalists, academics, and others skilled in exploring and enhancing the key elements of this unique relationship.

The Council's discussions of the implications of Korean unification and of problems in the Korean-US economic relationship are exactly the subjects it ought to be addressing—squarely and honestly—as its participants consider the quality of bilateral, Asia-Pacific, and international cooperation.

The enduring strength of the US-Korean alliance is apparent in more than traditional military terms, important as these ties remain. There are also the ever-deepening trade and investment ties as well as cooperation in UN peacekeeping activities from Haiti to Somalia to Cambodia. And there are shared democratic principles.

Peter Tarnoff is Undersecretary for Political Affairs, US State Department.

The US-Korean alliance is building into the future, as well as aiming for enduring peace and security on the Korea peninsula. Working together last October, the United States and South Korea collaborated on an agreement with North Korea that, when fully implemented, will end the threat of nuclear proliferation on the Korean peninsula.

By dealing constructively and conclusively with the nuclear threat, the agreed framework has set in motion currents that may ultimately lead to elimination of the fundamental threats to stability on the Korean peninsula and the establishment of a permanent and stable peace. Inter-Korean dialogue will allow the agreed framework to reach its full potential, namely a larger process of reconciliation. The United States looks to North Korea to fulfill its pledge promptly to resume constructive contacts with the South and welcomes the South's efforts to initiate dialogue.

Extraordinary events have carried us far from the state of gridlock on the nuclear issue that was evident scarcely a year ago. The importance that the international community attaches to North Korea's implementation of the agreed framework permits us a measure of hope that North Korea will see the agreement as a passport to better relations with many countries.

There are still major hurdles to clear, such as the Inter-Korea dialogue, which must resume. Without such dialogue it will become impossible to move the framework process forward. There is also the need to complete the detailed agreement for the supply of two light-water reactors to North Korea as a substitute for the dangerous technology it has agreed to give up.

The Republic of Korea has risen to the challenge of playing a central role in that important project. The United States welcomes South Korea's commitment, without which the agreed framework could not succeed. The "Korean model" reactors that will be provided are another example of the close US-Korean cooperation over many years. The ancestor of these reactors was an American model, but the current generation is designed and built in South Korea and contains well-tested, first-class technology and safety features. Similar reactors are already deployed in the United States throughout the Western world.

There has never been a more challenging, or hopeful, time on the Korean peninsula. The success of the joint efforts of the United States and the Republic of Korea with North Korea will have profound implications for overall security in Northeast Asia. They promise a historic shift that could redefine the parameters of security in a region that has been the center of struggles among great powers for centuries.

Implementation of the Geneva Agreement

RHA WOONG BAE

There has already been sufficient discussion on the North Korean nuclear issue at the conference earlier, so I would like to just briefly touch on a few of the matters with which I am most concerned in the implementation of the Geneva agreements. Despite some unsatisfactory aspects to these agreements, I believe that they provided a framework for a gradual resolution of the North Korean nuclear issue, and they contributed to reduced tensions, which peaked last June just before former President Jimmy Carter's visit to Pyongyang.

In this regard, I think it is undesirable to argue at this stage as to whether to accept or to reject the agreement. And it is also undesirable to consume too much energy scrutinizing the agreement simply in order to find its shortcomings. It is much more important to concentrate our efforts on how to use this agreed framework to settle the North Korean nuclear issue, to improve inter-Korea relations, and to ensure meaningful and lasting peace and security on the Korean peninsula.

My first concern is the resumption of North-South dialogue. We all agree that its resumption is the most important thing. South-North dialogue is indispensable for the smooth and effective implementation of the agreement. Without this dialogue, the agreement will virtually fail to be implemented. In fact, the most undesirable aspect of the Geneva agreement is that it was negotiated and signed between only the United States and North Korea. South Korea, although clearly a party with a strong interest, was completely excluded in the talks. This was quite

---

Rha Woong Bae is chairman of the Foreign Affairs Committee of the Korean National Assembly.

understandably rather difficult for the South Korean public to understand, particularly as the agreement calls for South Korea to make a significant financial contribution. Many Korean people believe that to resolve the North Korean nuclear issue and to ensure meaningful and lasting peace and security on the Korean peninsula, the United States should have included South Korea at the negotiating table from the beginning of the Geneva talks. Of course, North Korea would not accept it, but it was important for the United States to try.

Unfortunately, however, the prospect for the resumption of South-North dialogue is still cloudy. Despite our strenuous efforts, there has not been progress in inter-Korea relations because North Korea is stubbornly sticking to the strategy of negotiating with the United States and excluding South Korea. Under these circumstances, it would not be desirable for the United States to pursue speedy progress in its own relationship with North Korea. The prospects for South-North relations would become completely gloomy if North Korea were to become convinced that it could improve relations with the United States and address every issue regarding the Korean peninsula without reference to South Korea. Bearing this in mind, I would like to remind you that a hasty US rapprochement with North Korea may lead to the crippled implementation of the Geneva agreement by making North Korea less receptive to efforts at resuming the meaningful South-North dialogue.

The light-water reactor project constitutes a crucial part of the Geneva agreement's implementation. Every step in the provision of the light-water reactors should be used or leveraged to secure North Korea's full-fledged implementation of its obligations. Three basic requirements should be met before South Korea provides the financing for this project.

First, the South-North dialogue must be resumed. Second, the light-water reactors must be Korean. Third, South Korea should play a central role in the design and construction of the reactors. If these requirements are met, we are willing to assume due financial responsibility corresponding to our role. But if these requirements are not met and if South Korea continues to remain as an outsider in the implementation of the Geneva agreement, except for its financial contribution, the Korea National Assembly cannot guarantee support for the required financial contribution to the light-water reactor project.

As is true in the United States, our government needs the full understanding and support of our people in making a financial commitment to huge projects of this sort. In this regard, our government must prove that South Korea will play a central role that corresponds to the financial burden the South Korean people are asked to shoulder and that implementation of the agreement will improve inter-Korea relations.

I am glad to hear from Winston Lord, US assistant secretary of state for economic and business affairs, that it is the United States' firm position that the light-water reactors must come from Korea and that North

Korea will not get any reactors if it does not accept the Korean standard. Frankly, I was very worried about the stance the United States would take if North Korea were to continue rejecting South Korean reactors, and I am not entirely convinced that the United States is willing to break the Geneva agreement if North Korea fails to accept them. After all, the United States lacks leverage with North Korea, while North Korea has a great deal of leverage against South Korea. In this situation, it is certainly conceivable that the United States, interested as it is in ensuring the North's compliance with the nuclear nonproliferation treaty (NPT), would have to ask South Korea for some concessions regarding the reactors.

For example, it is possible that the United States might ask Korea to accept a finessing of the agreement so that the North Korean government can save face for domestic political purposes. For instance, the United States may ask Korea to refrain from referring to the reactors as being of Korean make, even though in actuality that's what they are. If South Korea accepts this concession, then it reinforces North Koreans' belief that they can settle matters on Korean peninsula by dealing directly with the United States while bypassing South Korea. If South Korea doesn't accept the concession, then the consequent bitter feelings between the United States and South Korea will eventually serve North Korea's strategy of driving a wedge between North and South, and the South and the United States.

Therefore, it is important that North Korea knows for certain that it will lose all its gains from the agreement if it does not accept the Korean-standard light-water reactors and if it does not resume a meaningful, sincere dialogue with South Korea. Of course, there is always the possibility that North Korea will leave the negotiating table and again begin playing its dangerous nuclear game if it does not get its way. The United States and South Korea must consult closely on policy and strategy to be ready for any future developments on the nuclear issue.

The other point I would like to make is that it would be most desirable and reasonable for the United States to play a more active financial role in the implementation of the agreement because it took such a strong initiative in negotiations for the Geneva agreement and also because it shares the benefits of the agreement—namely, a more favorable environment for extension of NPT by securing North Korean compliance.

US financial commitment will demonstrate its willingness to support the NPT and will help guarantee the smooth and faithful implementation of the agreement. If the United States were to bear all the costs, it would probably be acceptable to supply non-Korean light-water reactors. And if US were to make it clear it was willing to assume an active role in financing the light-water reactor project, other countries, including Japan, would be more likely to also provide support.

In conclusion, implementation of the Geneva agreement will be spread out over 10 years, and whether this will be smooth and faithful to the agreement remains an open question. The United States and South Korea must make every effort to ensure that North Korea fully carries out the agreement and that implementation provides the opportunity for improving inter-Korea relations. We especially must take advantage of the opportunities presented by the light-water reactor project.

South Korea will have to make every effort to provide a favorable environment for eventually transforming the present hostile state of South-North relations into a cooperative relationship. South Korea's decision to gradually delink economic from nuclear issues is one initiative to help achieve this. I do hope that North Korea will respond positively and accept the fact that the first step in maintaining peace and prosperity on the Korean peninsula is a sincere dialogue with South Korea. But to achieve this, South Korea needs the support of the United States.

US Congressional Agenda

DOUG BEREUTER

When the chairmanships of the five international relations subcommittees were determined, by virtue of my seniority I was able to choose second. Thus, I had a wide range of choices. I chose the Asia and Pacific Subcommittee because US relations with this region will have a substantial impact in shaping the security and economic health of our nation in the coming decades. Frankly, I leaped at the opportunity to have a hand in shaping and conducting oversight on US relations with Asia. And, of course, I take this responsibility quite seriously.

As chairman of the subcommittee, I have set three major priorities. I publicly spelled out these priorities for the first time on 9 February 1995, in a hearing where Assistant Secretary Winston Lord gave his inaugural testimony before our committee during the 104th Congress. Let me share my priorities with you this morning:

- The US military and naval presence and our security commitment to the region must be sustained and enhanced, both for the purpose of regional stability and in furtherance of our foreign policy goals and national interest. The United States has excellent friends and allies in Asia—most certainly including South Korea. We need to continue to work closely with our allies to achieve our common security objectives.

Doug Bereuter is chairman of the Committee on International Relations Subcommittee on Asia and the Pacific in the US House of Representatives.

- The United States must better focus and augment its resources and defend its interests to assure a larger and more competitive American economic presence and opportunities in the region in trade and other commercial areas.

- We must not neglect or downgrade the historic American commitment to our fundamental principles of democracy, pluralism, and human rights. At the same time, the United States must seek to enlarge and employ a more effective regional- and country-nuanced array of our own and multilateral policies, programs, and techniques to foster these principles in the region.

I believe it is fair to say that these priorities differ in some important ways from the agendas of my predecessors as chairman of the Asia and Pacific Subcommittee. For example, I intend to place a higher priority on the economic aspect of the US relationship with Asia. Given the prominence of trade and economic issues, I believe this is only appropriate. I intend to be very aggressive in doing what I can to expose the tariff quotas and the plethora of nontariff barriers that continue to frustrate US exporters in Asia. I will return to this issue in a few moments.

I also expect to do what I can to ensure even greater US emphasis on the emerging multilateral institutions of Asia, including APEC and the ASEAN Regional Forum (ARF), which adds a security dimension to the ASEAN framework.

As an aside, let me say that I am pleased and privileged to have, as a distinguished member of my subcommittee, the first Korean-American member of the House of Representatives—Mr. Jay Kim. Obviously, he has unique expertise and insights regarding US relations with South Korea and Northeast Asia, and I look forward to working with him in the 104th Congress.

US–South Korean Strategic Relationship

Let me turn to some specific observations regarding the US relationship with Korea, particularly from the view of the House of Representatives. Immediately after the end of the Cold War, you will recall that there was some discussion about the size and duration of America's continued military presence on the Korean peninsula.

Indeed, at the same time that the Soviet Union was collapsing, there was some simultaneous movement in relations between North and South Korea. In retrospect, there clearly were some unrealistic assumptions regarding future prospects for peace and security in Northeast Asia. But the hope was there for a marked improvement in North-South relations. In 1991 President Bush had announced the withdrawal of nuclear weapons in South Korea. This was also the time when the United States and the Republic of Korea had concluded a new Status of Forces Agreement that addressed long-standing Korean complaints regarding the inequity of treatment of US and Korean troops stationed in Korea. There was the 1992 Agreement on Reconciliation, Nonaggression, Cooperation and Exchanges. The agreements called for the holding of a North-South summit, establishment of North-South liaison offices, and agreement on a series of confidence-building measures. It was in this context that, in the late 1980s and early 1990s, some members of Congress, including former Chairman Stephen Solarz, supported proposals to reduce the US military presence on the Korean peninsula.

Clearly, hopes for progress with the North were not realized, and for over a year now we have faced the confrontation over the North's nuclear program. This confrontation with North Korea—where inspectors of the International Atomic Energy Agency have been denied the right to verify Pyongyang's nuclear activities—is perhaps the most serious security threat that the United States currently faces. I'm sure that most members of Congress do not underestimate the risk of confrontation and escalation.

In the House of Representatives, there is great frustration with the so-called Agreed Framework on Denuclearization of the Korean Peninsula that was reached last October. It is particularly troubling because we have known this crisis was brewing for many years. We have had reasonably good intelligence on certain important aspects of North Korean nuclear activities, but the Clinton administration, and indeed the Bush administration before it, delayed in taking decisive action. As a result, we now have few attractive options. It may be that the agreed framework will be endorsed, or at least not rejected, by Congress, but only after very careful scrutiny—if the administration answers some very tough questions on the agreement and its actions.

The Senate already has held hearings on the agreed framework and the creation of the Korean Economic Development Office (KEDO). In the International Relations Committee, I will be holding classified briefings and open hearings on the agreed framework in the very near future, and I expect a very spirited exchange with Ambassador-at-Large Robert Gallucci.

Congress is well aware that Pyongyang is trying to drive a wedge between the United States and its South Korean allies. I will tell you that I will do everything in my power as subcommittee chairman to prevent this from occurring. US–South Korean relations must not be held hostage to the brinksmanship of the North Korean thugs. In that regard, Senators Frank Murkowski and Chuck Robb have introduced a resolution that expresses the sense of Congress that the agreed framework should be linked to substantive progress in the dialogue between North and South Korea. The point is that North Korea undertook an obligation in 1992 to pursue a wide range of bilateral contacts with the

South. As we all know, North Korea has since reneged on this obligation.

It seems to me that we should expect the North to honor its obligations. Establishing such a basic set of conditions certainly would reduce the prospect of a wedge being driven between the United States and South Korea. This is an area that the subcommittee will closely scrutinize.

Trade and Investment

Turning to another subject, I would certainly be remiss if I failed to mention a quite contentious trade issue between the United States and Korea that has had a significant effect on the farmers and cattle producers among my constituents in Nebraska's 1st District. I do not cite this trade dispute only for parochial reasons, for I believe it is symptomatic of many of our current and future trade problems with the Republic of Korea and various other countries in the Pacific Rim region.

In November, US Trade Representative Mickey Kantor initiated a section 301 investigation of Korea's practices regarding the importation of US beef and pork. This section 301 action is only the latest in an exhausting series of bilateral meetings since 1988 with that country over its cumbersome and discriminatory regulatory barriers to US meat products.

Throughout five years of negotiations, the Republic of Korea has broken three separate written promises and forced the United States to take this trade dispute before a GATT panel to obtain a favorable panel ruling. Nevertheless, the Republic of Korea maintains the following regulatory barriers to US meat exports:

- outdated, scientifically unsupported, discriminatory shelf-life standards;

- excessively long inspection procedures;

- contract tender procedures that prevent US producers from meaningfully participating in the bidding process;

- local processing and repackaging requirements that severely and unfairly disadvantage American exporters;

- discriminatory fixed-weight requirements;

- dual standards for residue testing.

As Deputy USTR Charlene Barshefsky testified before our subcommittee's hearing, while formal barriers to imports have fallen in Korea, "new, more subtle barriers have effectively prevented the liberalization sioned under the major trade policy initiatives of the late 1980s. Korea's nontariff trade barriers are often compared to those of Japan's ten years ago."

Obviously, the Uruguay Round and Korea's membership in the world trade body will provide substantial opportunities for US goods and services exporters. As pointed out by Undersecretary of Commerce for International Trade Jeffrey Garten, Korea, as the 13th largest economy in the world, is one of the 11 big emerging markets (BEMs) for US exporters. However, I remain very concerned that nearly every industry and business sector, except those being outright "courted" by the Republic of Korea, will face a similar set of regulatory barriers at each and every turn as they try to enter this incredibly frustrating market. This is an intolerable situation.

I presume that if we were to put US bankers and US cattle producers together, they could agree on at least one thing: Korea is a very difficult market to crack. Again, this is but one illustration of a very big and general problem for American exporters.

Conclusions

I'm aware of the fact that I have outlined quite an extensive agenda for improving US-Korean relations. The United States and the Republic of Korea are important allies and have a wide range of shared interests.

There also are very important trade and commercial issues that need to be resolved in our bilateral relations. America has been tolerant about Korea's nontariff trade barriers for far too long. Now that the Cold War is over, we can and should demand an end to the unfair treatment for the American side in this bilateral relationship.

I do approach the chairmanship of the Asia and Pacific Subcommittee with good intent to fairly address the remaining difficulties between Korea and the United States so as to advance our friendship and our security relationship. I will try to build on the shared values that have arisen from the long and positive relationship with Korea.

Conference Participants

Ronald Aqua
United States-Japan Foundation

Taeho Bark
Korea Institute for International
  Economic Policy

Charlene Barshefsky
Office of the US Trade Representative

Thomas Bayard
Institute for International Economics

Douglas Bereuter
US House of Representatives

C. Fred Bergsten
Institute for International Economics

Daniel Bob
Office of Senator Roth

David Brown
Department of State

Sokan Chang
Ministry of Trade, Industry and Energy

Soon Sung Cho
National Assembly

Yoon Je Cho
Ministry of Finance and Economy

Chang Yoon Choi
Korea Foundation

Myung Gun Choo
Sejong Institution

Charles Dallara
Institute of International Finance

John Eby
Ford Motor

Kimberly Ann Elliott
Institute for International Economics

Richard Finn
Senate Armed Services Committee

Jeffrey Frankel
Institute for International Economics

Michael Gadbaw
General Electric

Robert Hall
National Retail Federation

Lisa Heyes
Asia Foundation

Jim Hoagland
Washington Post

Peter Howell
Citibank

John Huang
Department of Commerce

Thomas Hubbard
Department of State

Ann Kambara
Department of State

Dae Joong Kim
Chosun Ilbo

Hakjoon Kim
Former Senior Secretary
  to the President for Political Affairs

Hyun Chul Kim
Sammi Group

Kyung Won Kim
Former Korean Ambassador to US

Sam Hoon Kim
Ministry of Foreign Affairs

Suk Joon Kim
Ssangyong Business Group

Wan Soon Kim
Korea Trade Commission

Young Hie Kim
Samsung Economics Institute

Craig Kramer
Office of Congressman Levin

Lawrence Krause
University of California, San Diego

Robert Kyle
National Economic Council/National
  Security Council

Dong-Bok Lee
George Washington University

Jae Seung Lee
Hankook Ilbo

Young Sun Lee
Yonsei University

James Lilley
American Enterprise Institute

Winston Lord
Department of State

Christine Lund
Office of the US Trade
  Representative

Sean Mulvaney
Office of Congressman Kolbe

Ron Neal
Motorola

Marcus Noland
Institute for International Economics

Deanna Okun
Office of Senator Murkowski

Lionel Olmer
Paul Weiss Rifkin Warthon
  & Garrison

Douglas Paal
Asia Pacific Policy Center

Ungsuh Kenneth Park
Samsung Petrochemical

Woong-Bae Rha
National Assembly

Stanley Roth
National Security Council

Il SaKong
Institute for Global Economics

Jeffrey Schott
Institute for International Economics

Drew Setter
Office of Congressman Levin

Paul Simon
United States Senate

Hak Kyu Sohn
National Assembly

Joseph Stiglitz
Council of Economic Advisers

Daniel Tarullo
Department of State

Robert Warne
Korea Economic Institute of America

Won Young Yon
Ministry of Finance and Economy

Han-Soo Yoo
POSCO Research Insitute

Young Suk Yoon
Daewoo Heavy Industries

Soogil Young
Korea Transport Institute

Robert Zoellick
Federal National Mortgage
    Association

Observers: Young Mo Ahn
Korea Foundation

Inbom Choi
Korea Institute for International
    Economic Policy

Todd Snyder
Department of the Treasury

Coordinators: Tae Hyun Ha
Institute for Global Economics

Il Boong Park
Institute for Global Economics

Kyoung Chul Park
Korea Foundation

Other Publications from the
Institute for International Economics

POLICY ANALYSES IN INTERNATIONAL ECONOMICS Series

BOOKS

IMF Conditionality
John Williamson, editor/*1983*
ISBN cloth 0-88132-006-4   695 pp.

Trade Policy in the 1980s
William R. Cline, editor/*1983*
(out of print)   ISBN cloth 0-88132-008-1   810 pp.
ISBN paper 0-88132-031-5   810 pp.

Subsidies in International Trade
Gary Clyde Hufbauer and Joanna Shelton Erb/*1984*
ISBN cloth 0-88132-004-8   299 pp.

International Debt: Systemic Risk and Policy Response
William R. Cline/*1984*
ISBN cloth 0-88132-015-3   336 pp.

Trade Protection in the United States: 31 Case Studies
Gary Clyde Hufbauer, Diane E. Berliner, and Kimberly Ann Elliott/*1986*
(out of print)   ISBN paper 0-88132-040-4   371 pp.

Toward Renewed Economic Growth in Latin America
Bela Balassa, Gerardo M. Bueno, Pedro-Pablo Kuczynski,
and Mario Henrique Simonsen/*1986*
(out of stock)   ISBN paper 0-88132-045-5   205 pp.

Capital Flight and Third World Debt
Donald R. Lessard and John Williamson, editors/*1987*
(out of print)   ISBN paper 0-88132-053-6   270 pp.

**The Canada-United States Free Trade Agreement:
The Global Impact**
Jeffrey J. Schott and Murray G. Smith, editors/*1988*
ISBN paper 0-88132-073-0   211 pp.

World Agricultural Trade: Building a Consensus
William M. Miner and Dale E. Hathaway, editors/*1988*
ISBN paper 0-88132-071-3   226 pp.

Japan in the World Economy
Bela Balassa and Marcus Noland/*1988*
ISBN paper 0-88132-041-2   306 pp.

America in the World Economy: A Strategy for the 1990s
C. Fred Bergsten/*1988*
ISBN cloth 0-88132-089-7   235 pp.
ISBN paper 0-88132-082-X   235 pp.

Managing the Dollar: From the Plaza to the Louvre
Yoichi Funabashi/*1988, 2d ed. 1989*
ISBN paper 0-88132-097-8   307 pp.

United States External Adjustment and the World Economy
William R. Cline/*May 1989*
ISBN paper 0-88132-048-X   392 pp.

Free Trade Areas and U.S. Trade Policy
Jeffrey J. Schott, editor/*May 1989*
ISBN paper 0-88132-094-3   400 pp.

Dollar Politics: Exchange Rate Policymaking in the United States
I. M. Destler and C. Randall Henning/*September 1989*
(out of print)   ISBN paper 0-88132-079-X   192 pp.

Latin American Adjustment: How Much Has Happened?
John Williamson, editor/*April 1990*
                            ISBN paper 0-88132-125-7   480 pp.

The Future of World Trade in Textiles and Apparel
William R. Cline/*1987, 2d ed. June 1990*
                            ISBN paper 0-88132-110-9   344 pp.

**Completing the Uruguay Round: A Results-Oriented Approach
to the GATT Trade Negotiations**
Jeffrey J. Schott, editor/*September 1990*
                            ISBN paper 0-88132-130-3   256 pp.

Economic Sanctions Reconsidered (in two volumes)
   Economic Sanctions Reconsidered: Supplemental Case Histories
   Gary Clyde Hufbauer, Jeffrey J. Schott, and Kimberly Ann Elliott/*1985, 2d ed.
    December 1990*
                            ISBN cloth 0-88132-115-X   928 pp.
                            ISBN paper 0-88132-105-2   928 pp.

   Economic Sanctions Reconsidered: History and Current Policy
   Gary Clyde Hufbauer, Jeffrey J. Schott, and Kimberly Ann Elliott/*December 1990*
                            ISBN cloth 0-88132-136-2   288 pp.
                            ISBN paper 0-88132-140-0   288 pp.

Pacific Basin Developing Countries: Prospects for the Future
Marcus Noland/*January 1991*
(out of print)   ISBN cloth 0-88132-141-9   250 pp.
                            ISBN paper 0-88132-081-1   250 pp.

Currency Convertibility in Eastern Europe
John Williamson, editor/*October 1991*
                            ISBN cloth 0-88132-144-3   396 pp.
                            ISBN paper 0-88132-128-1   396 pp.

International Adjustment and Financing: The Lessons of 1985-1991
C. Fred Bergsten, editor/*January 1992*
                            ISBN paper 0-88132-112-5   336 pp.

North American Free Trade: Issues and Recommendations
Gary Clyde Hufbauer and Jeffrey J. Schott/*April 1992*
                            ISBN cloth 0-88132-145-1   392 pp.
                            ISBN paper 0-88132-120-6   392 pp.

Narrowing the U.S. Current Account Deficit
Allen J. Lenz/*June 1992*
(out of print)   ISBN cloth 0-88132-148-6   640 pp.
                            ISBN paper 0-88132-103-6   640 pp.

The Economics of Global Warming
William R. Cline/*June 1992*
                            ISBN cloth 0-88132-150-8   416 pp.
                            ISBN paper 0-88132-132-X   416 pp.

U.S. Taxation of International Income: Blueprint for Reform
Gary Clyde Hufbauer, assisted by Joanna M. van Rooij/*October 1992*
                            ISBN cloth 0-88132-178-8   304 pp.
                            ISBN paper 0-88132-134-6   304 pp.

Currencies and Politics in the United States, Germany, and Japan
C. Randall Henning/*September 1994*
ISBN paper 0-88132-127-3   432 pp.

Estimating Equilibrium Exchange Rates
John Williamson, editor/*September 1994*
ISBN paper 0-88132-076-5   320 pp.

Managing the World Economy: Fifty Years After Bretton Woods
Peter B. Kenen, editor/*September 1994*
ISBN paper 0-88132-212-1   448 pp.

Reciprocity and Retaliation in U.S. Trade Policy
Thomas O. Bayard and Kimberly Ann Elliott/*September 1994*
ISBN paper 0-88132-084-6   528 pp.

The Uruguay Round: An Assessment
Jeffrey J. Schott, assisted by Johanna W. Buurman/*November 1994*
ISBN paper 0-88132-206-7   240 pp.

Measuring the Costs of Protection in Japan
Yoko Sazanami, Shujiro Urata, and Hiroki Kawai/*January 1995*
ISBN paper 0-88132-211-3   96 pp.

Foreign Direct Investment in the United States, Third Edition
Edward M. Graham and Paul R. Krugman/*January 1995*
ISBN paper 0-88132-204-0   232 pp.

The Political Economy of Korea-United States Cooperation
C. Fred Bergsten and Il SaKong, editors/*February 1995*
ISBN paper 0-88132-213-X   128 pp.

International Debt Reexamined
William R. Cline/*February 1995*
ISBN paper 0-88132-083-8   560 pp.

American Trade Politics, Third Edition
I. M. Destler/*April 1995*
ISBN paper 0-88132-215-6   360 pp.

Managing Official Export Credits: The Quest for a Global Regime
John E. Ray/*July 1995*
ISBN paper 0-88132-207-5   344 pp.

Asia Pacific Fusion: Japan's Role in APEC
Yoichi Funabashi/*October 1995*
ISBN paper 0-88132-224-5   312 pp.

Korea-United States Cooperation in the New World Order
C. Fred Bergsten and Il SaKong, editors/*February 1996*
ISBN paper 0-88132-226-1   144 pp.

SPECIAL REPORTS

1   Promoting World Recovery: A Statement on Global Economic Strategy by Twenty-six Economists from Fourteen Countries/*December 1982*
(out of print)   ISBN paper 0-88132-013-7   45 pp.

2   Prospects for Adjustment in Argentina, Brazil, and Mexico: Responding to the Debt Crisis   (out of print)
John Williamson, editor/*June 1983*   ISBN paper 0-88132-016-1   71 pp.

3   Inflation and Indexation: Argentina, Brazil, and Israel
John Williamson, editor/*March 1985*   ISBN paper 0-88132-037-4   191 pp.

4   Global Economic Imbalances
C. Fred Bergsten, editor/*March 1986*   ISBN cloth 0-88132-038-2   126 pp.
ISBN paper 0-88132-042-0   126 pp.

WORKS IN PROGRESS

Mismanaging the World Economy: The Demise of the G7
C. Fred Bergsten and C. Randall Henning

Trade, Jobs, and Income Distribution
William R. Cline

Trade and Labor Standards
Kimberly Ann Elliott and Richard Freeman

Regionalism and Globalism in the World Economic System
Jeffrey A. Frankel

Transatlantic Free Trade Agreement
Ellen Frost

Overseeing Global Capital Markets
Morris Goldstein and Peter Garber

Global Corporations and National Governments
Edward M. Graham

Global Competition Policy
Edward M. Graham and J. David Richardson

Toward an Asia Pacific Economic Community?
Gary Clyde Hufbauer and Jeffrey J. Schott

The Economics of Korean Unification
Marcus Noland

The Case for Trade: A Modern Reconsideration
J. David Richardson

The Future of the World Trading System
John Whalley, in collaboration with Colleen Hamilton

For orders outside the US and Canada please contact:

Longman Group UK Ltd.   Telephone Orders: 0279 623923
PO Box 88, Fourth Avenue   Fax: 0279 453450   Telex: 81259
Harlow, Essex CM 19 5SR UK

Canadian customers can order from the Institute or from either:

RENOUF BOOKSTORE   LA LIBERTÉ
1294 Algoma Road   3020 chemin Sainte-Foy
Ottawa, Ontario K1B 3W8   Quebec G1X 3V6
Telephone: (613) 741-4333   Telephone: (418) 658-3763
Fax: (613) 741-5439   Fax: (800) 567-5449

Visit our website at: http://www.iie.com   E-mail address: orders@iie.com